New E1

Haunted Lighthouses

Haunted Ships, Forts and the Unexplainable

ISBN 978-1-935616-18-4

For additional copies or more information, please contact:

Salty Pilgrim Press
17 Causeway Street
Millis, MA 02054 USA
1 508 794-1200

captain@saltypilgrim.com
www.SaltyPilgrim.com

Theodore Parker Burbank

Dedication

I am happy to dedicate this book to my niece Doreen and her son Eric who are both dedicated ghost hunters and have encouraged me greatly in this undertaking.

Theodore Parker Burbank

THE LIGHTHOUSE

by Henry Wadsworth Longfellow

The rocky ledge runs far into the sea, and on its outer point, some miles away, the lighthouse lifts its massive masonry, A pillar of fire by night, of cloud by day.

Even at this distance I can see the tides, Up heaving, break unheard along its base, A speechless wrath, that rises and subsides in the white tip and tremor of the face.

And as the evening darkens, lo! how bright, through the deep purple of the twilight air, Beams forth the sudden radiance of its light, with strange, unearthly splendor in the glare!

No one alone: from each projecting cape And perilous reef along the ocean's verge, Starts into life a dim, gigantic shape, Holding its lantern o'er the restless surge.

Like the great giant Christopher it stands Upon the brink of the tempestuous wave, Wading far out among the rocks and sands, The night o'er taken mariner to save.

And the great ships sail outward and returnBending and bowing o'er the billowy swells, And ever joyful, as they see it burn they wave their silent welcome and farewells.

They come forth from the darkness, and their sails Gleam for a moment only in the blaze, And eager faces, as the light unveils Gaze at the tower, and vanish while they gaze.

The mariner remembers when a child, on his first voyage, he saw it fade and sink And when returning from adventures wild, He saw it rise again o'er ocean's brink.

Steadfast, serene, immovable, the same, Year after year, through all the silent night Burns on forevermore that quenchless flame, Shines on that inextinguishable light!

It sees the ocean to its bosom clasp The rocks and sea-sand with the kiss of peace: It sees the wild winds lift it in their grasp, And hold it up, and shake it like a fleece.

The startled waves leap over it; the storm Smites it with all the scourges of the rain, And steadily against its solid form press the great shoulders of the hurricane.

The sea-bird wheeling round it, with the din of wings and winds and solitary cries, Blinded and maddened by the light within, Dashes himself against the glare, and dies.

A new Prometheus, chained upon the rock, Still grasping in his hand the fire of love, it does not hear the cry, nor heed the shock, but hails the mariner with words of love.

"Sail on!" it says: "sail on, ye stately ships! And with your floating bridge the ocean span;Be mine to guard this light from all eclipse.Be yours to bring man neared unto man."

Table of Content

What is a Ghost	1
Light Characteristics	10
Lighthouse Markings	14
A Ghostly Quiz	16

Connecticut:

New London Ledge Lighthouse	21
Penfield Reef Lighthouse	25
Southeast Light, Block Island	29
Stratford Shoals Light	33
The Ghost Ship of New Haven	37
Ghost Ship *Palatine*	*39*

Rhode Island:

Fort Adams	45
Fort Wetherhill	49

Massachusetts:

North Shore

Bakers Island Light	55
Bird Island Light	58
Eastern Point Light	61
Ghost Ship of Salem	67

Boston Harbor

Boston Light	69
Nixes Mate Island Beacon	75
Long Island Light - Fort Strong	79
USS Constitution	83
USS Salem – 139	87
Castle Island	91
Fort Warren	93

South Shore

Minot Light	99
Plymouth Lighthouse - Brown's Bank	111
Scituate Light - Cohasset Shipwrecks	121

Cape Cod
> Nauset Light   127
> Race Point Light   133

New Hampshire:
> Portsmouth Harbor Lighthouse   139
> Fort Constitution a/k/a Fort William & Mary

Maine:

South Coast
> Cape Neddick Light   145
> Boon Island Light   149
> Ghost Ship of Harpswell   153
> Wood Island Light   157
> Ram Island Light   161
> Portland Head Light   165
> Fort Williams Park   169

Mid Coast
> Hendrick Light   175
> Marshall Point Light   179
> Matinicus Rock Lighthouse   181
> Fort William Henry   187
> Pemaquid Point Light   191
> Sequin Island Light   195
> Owl's Head Light   201
> Fort Knox   207
> Jonathan Buck Monument   213

Bold Coast
> Mount Desert Light   219
> Prospect Harbor Light   223
> Winter Harbor Light   227
> West Quoddy Light   231
> Quiz Answers   233

What is a Ghost?

Are they real? - The Many Theories and Types

People around the world and in every culture have recorded personal interactions and experiences with ghosts for thousands of years. But just what is a ghost anyway? There are many types of ghosts and several conflicting theories as to what ghosts are. Other names for ghosts include: specter, phantom, apparition or spook. All are thought to be the spirit of a dead person or animal that make themselves know to the living in one way or another. We will explore the most common theories and describe the most prevalent types of ghosts.

The Number One Theory
Ghosts are the Spirits of Dead People or Animals

Many religions, including Judeo and Christian faiths, believe that when we die, our spirit continues on. Believe in a life hereafter be it heaven or hell is found in most mainstream religion doctrine. Ghosts are among the most widely believed of paranormal phenomena: Millions of people are interested in ghosts, and a surprisingly large number will admit to experiencing unexplainable non-earthly encounters. A 2005 Gallup poll found that 37 percent of

Theodore Parker Burbank

Americans believe in haunted houses and nearly half believe in ghosts.

Albert Einstein suggested a scientific basis for the reality of ghosts; *"If energy cannot be created or destroyed but only change form, what happens to our body's energy when we die? Could that energy somehow be manifested as a ghost?*

Messengers
The most common ghostly encounter is with the spirit of a recently departed loved one. These encounters, although surprising and somewhat startling, are usually comforting and seldom recur. On the other hand, witnessing a spirit you did not known in the living world is hardly comforting. This kind of ghost may be the most common.

These spirits usually appear shortly after their deaths to people close to them. They are aware of their deaths and can interact with the living. They most often bring messages of comfort to their loved ones, to say that they are well and happy, and not to grieve for them. These ghosts appear briefly and usually only once. It is as if they intentionally return with their messages for the express purpose of helping the living cope with their loss.

Lauren Forcella at Paranormal Investigations calls these ghosts Crisis Apparitions. *"This category commonly involves one-time visits to someone with whom the apparition has close emotional ties. Though the encounter usually seems to be a type of farewell, sometimes important and useful information is relayed to the 'viewer.' Though dying is the most common crisis, other life-threatening situations can also trigger apparitional visits."*

The "Lost" Ghost
Part of the difficulty in investigating ghosts is that there is not one universally agreed-upon definition of what a ghost is. Some believe that they are spirits of the dead who for whatever reason get "lost" on their way to The Other Side; others claim that ghosts are instead telepathic entities projected into the world from our minds.

This popular type of ghosts is the thought to be the spirit of a person or persons that died and for some reason are "stuck" between this plane of existence and the next. Usually their death was traumatic or sudden often resulting from a tragedy. Many psychics believe that such earth-bound spirits don't know they are dead.

Veteran ghost hunter Hans Holzer wrote:

*"A ghost is a human being who has passed out of the physical body, usually in a
traumatic state and is not aware
usually of his true condition. We are all spirits encased in a physical body. At
the time of passing, our spirit body continues into the next dimension. A ghost,
on the other hand, due to trauma, is stuck in our physical world
and needs to be released to go on."*

Intelligent Hauntings

These ghosts haunt the scenes of their deaths or at locations that
were pleasant or important to them in life. Very often, these types
of ghosts are aware of the living and are able to interact with them.
This type of ghost often will give warning of danger to the living.
Ghost of the lighthouse dog that still rings the warning bell in times
of peril is an example of this type of ghost. Some psychics claim to
be able to communicate with them.

Recording Ghosts or Residual Hauntings

This type of ghost is believed to be recordings of the past that
somehow got stamped into the environment and are actually
recordings or remnants of the past. Proponents of this theory
report: "What we recognize as a ghost is really just history playing
back. There is no spirit present at all. It is like watching a movie."

Paranormal investigators say that past events somehow record
themselves into the environment. An example would be battlefields
such as Gettysburg where ghosts are reportedly seen going about
their business just as though the war was still raging. A child's
laughter is heard in a dead child's former playroom. The lighthouse
keeper's wife continually playing her piano using her only piece of
sheet music fits this category of ghost.

Strange Nation in "What Is a Ghost?" explains Residual Hauntings:
*"A traumatic moment in time leaves an indelible impression on the building or
area replaying itself for eternity. This could be anything from a 'glimpse of the
past' - a recreation of some traumatic or emotion-laden event - to footsteps up and
down a hallway."* Lauren Forcella writes -*"How and why past events are
recorded and replayed repetitiously is not understood. Whatever the actual
mechanism, it apparently possesses longevity as the encore performances of a*

3

haunting can continue for decades or longer. Generally, the haunting is a fragment or portion of an actual event."

This type of ghost does not interact with nor does it seem to be aware of the living.

Non-Visible/Audible Ghostly Encounters
Most Common Signs From Departed Loved Ones

Departed love ones may never be far away from us even though they are on "The Other Side." They may not actually appear to us but will leave signs for us to recognize they are with us and love us. We may notice these signs if we are not too busy with our everyday activities and routines. The signs our loved ones give us most often are:

Come through as an animal. Our loved ones are able to use their energy to use an animal, such as a butterfly, ladybug, bird, or dragonfly – for a brief period of time. The animal does something it usually would not do, such as land on us, peck at our window, scream at us, etc.

The visitation of a cardinal is said to be a representative of a loved one who has passed. When you see one, it means they are visiting you. They usually show up when you most need them or miss them. They also make an appearance during times of celebration as well as despair to let you know they will always be with you.

4

Place common objects such as feathers, coins, or rocks in our path. Our loved ones like to place things over and over again in our path that were significant to them.

Give off fragrances. We can often tell our deceased loved ones are around us when we smell their perfume, flowers, cigar or cigarette smoke, or any other familiar smell they had. There is usually no logical explanation of why the smell is there.

Make songs come on at the perfect time. We know they are around when their favorite songs come on at the right time with the exact words we need to hear. Often the same song is played in many different places.

Come to us in dreams. One of the easiest ways for them to come through to us is in our dreams. All we need to do is to ask them to come, and they *will*. However, we should ask them to wake us up after they come, or else we will not remember the dream.

A dream that is a true visitation will be very peaceful and we will *know* it is truly our loved one. We will remember this type of dream in detail many years later. (On the other hand, a subconscious dream may be frightening or feel bad. This type of dream is *not* your loved one.)

Show us the same numbers over and over. They loved to give us numbers that are relevant to them or you, such as birthdates, anniversaries – or repeating numbers, such as 1111, 2222, 3333, etc. These numbers may appear on clocks, billboards, or any other familiar place.

Allow us to feel peaceful for no reason. When our loved ones are in the room, they usually make us feel so loved and at peace. It usually happens at the most unsuspecting time, so there is no logical explanation for our sudden bliss.

Place thoughts in our head. Because they in spirit form, our loved ones don't have an audible voice. Therefore, they give us messages telepathically. Pay attention to thoughts that just "pop" into your head. We can tell the difference between our thoughts and theirs by backtracking our thoughts.

If you can find the thought that triggered the thought of your loved one, it is probably *your* thought. If something your loved one would say just *pops* in your head for no reason, it is probably him or her speaking directly to you!

Play with electricity. They turn electricity on and off. They like to flicker lights, turn the television and radio on and off, and make appliances beep for no apparent reason.

Make buzzing noises in our ears. Because our loved ones speak to us on a different, higher frequency, we may hear ringing in our ears when they are trying to get our attention. This is a sign telling you to listen to what they are saying.

The list can go on and on, but these are the most common ways they let us know they are around.

Poltergeists

This type of haunting is the most feared because it has the ability to affect our physical world. A poltergeist (German for "noisy ghost") is a type of ghost or other supernatural being supposedly responsible for physical disturbances such as loud noises and objects moved around or destroyed. Most accounts of poltergeists describe movement or levitation of objects, such as furniture and cutlery, or noises such as knocking on doors. Poltergeists have also been claimed to be capable of pinching, biting, hitting and tripping people.

Poltergeists occupy numerous niches in cultural folklore, and have traditionally been described as troublesome spirits who haunt a particular person instead of a specific location. Such alleged poltergeist manifestations have been reported in many cultures and countries including the United States, Japan, Brazil, Australia, and most European nations, with early accounts dating back to the 1st century. The first reported poltergeist was in Germany in 856 AD.

They take our possessions and hide them, only to return them later. They turn on faucets, slam doors, turn lights on and off, and flush toilets. They throw things across rooms. They have been known to pull on people's clothing or hair. The malevolent ones even slap and scratch the living. It is because of these sometimes "mean-spirited" manifestations that poltergeists are considered by some investigators to be demonic in nature.

Other investigators, however, believe that ghosts do not cause poltergeist activity, but is actually psycho kinesis brought on by people under stress. Lauren Forcella writes: *"During a poltergeist experience the agent, in an attempt to relieve emotional stress, unknowingly causes the physical disturbances using mental forces. The mental mechanism that allows the poltergeist agent to unconsciously cause these physical disturbances is called psycho kinesis."*

Shadow People

A shadow person (also known as a shadow figure, shadow being or black mass) is the perception of a patch of shadow as a living, humanoid figure, particularly as interpreted by believers in the supernatural as the presence of a malevolent entity.

At first, they appear only out of the corner of your eye, furtively darting out of view when you turn to look straight at them, but are now gone. Did you really see them?

Shaking the image out of your head, you assume that it was some peculiar anomaly of your eyesight, however the feeling still lingers that someone continues to watch you. Sometimes it appears as the mere silhouette of a person, usually male, but generally lacking any other characteristics of gender. However, in no way does the description end there.

There are "hatted" shadow beings, hooded shadows, cloaked ones, and solid or wispy, smoky types. Some are seen only from the waist up. Others clearly have legs that are seen fleeing from their observers. They dart into corners, through walls, into closets, or behind television sets, bushes, and buildings. Sometimes they simply fade into the dark recesses of the night. Lacking in the description is one common denominator unifying the many different types of shadow people that enter our world, except that they are "intensely dark". Even then, there are exceptions.

More Theories

Ghosts are From Another Dimension.

Theoretical physicists theorize there may be many different universes, dimensions and timelines besides the one we live in. They speculate that ghosts are not spirits of the departed but instead, are inter-dimensional beings; entities actually living in a different time and place.

If other beings are accidentally crossing into our dimension, do we ever cross into theirs? Maybe occurrences such as astral projection and lucid dreaming can be linked to short trips into separate but similar dimensions.

Ghosts are Actually Angels and Demons

Another school of thought states there are no such things as ghosts. What we believe to be ghosts, they insist, are either angels attempting to protect us or, demons attempting to trick us.

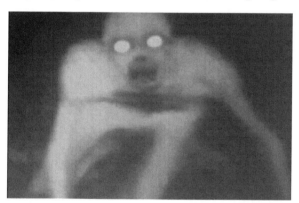

Guardian Angels who are believed to "looking down upon you" making sure you're safe fit this description. "The devil made me do it" might be explained by this theory.

Ghosts are a Figment of our Imagination

Out brains may be more powerful than we realize. Many simply dismiss the concept of ghosts as merely a figment of one's imagination. "It's all in your head" they say; a very convenient and easy way to completely dismiss the subject. Science has yet to fully understand the powers of the human mind.

Are you more or less comforted to know that the apparition you've been seeing wandering about your home is a projection of a family member's sub consciousness rather than a real ghost?

Light Characteristic

In order that mariners could determine which light they are viewing, different lights use different colors, frequencies of flash and light patterns. Each lighthouse beacon is unique thereby allowing mariners to distinguish one lighthouse from another at night.

Symbols and abbreviations for light characteristics:

Description	Characteristic	Chart Abbreviation
Alternating		Alt. R.W.G.
Fixed		F.
Flashing		Fl.
Group flashing		Gp Fl.(2)
Occulting		Occ.
Group occulting		Gp Occ(3)
Quick flashing		Qk.Fl.
Very quick flashing		V.Qk.Fl.
Isophase		Iso.
Morse		Mo.(letter)

Three *main factors* that make up a beacon's unique characteristic:

1) **Color:** The color of a beacon's light is used to communicate important information and/or identify the purpose of the lighthouse

> **White** - Used to identify navigational beacons. (W)
> **Red** - Often used to identify dangerous areas and to warn ships that can see the red light to turn away. Red is also used to identify the starboard (right) side of a channel. (R)
> **Green** – Often used to identify safe waters. Green is also used to identify the port (left) side of a channel. (G)
> **Yellow** – Infrequently used (Y)

2) **Flash Pattern:** A beacon may remain steady or possess a unique flash pattern.

The most common patterns include:

> **Fixed** - A continuous steady light that does not flash. (F.)
> **Fixed Flashing** - A single flash. (F. Fl.)

> **Group Flashing** - A beacon that features a group of flashes over a specific period of time. (Gr. Fl.)

3) **Time** - The amount of time it takes for a specific flash pattern to occur varies from one lighthouse to another. Most flash patterns take between 15 and 60 seconds to complete before repeating themselves

Other Factors:

Occulting light -An occulting light is a rhythmic light in which the total duration of light in each period is clearly longer than the total duration of darkness and in which the intervals of darkness (occultations) are all of equal duration. Like a flashing light, it can be used for a single occulting light that exhibits only single occultations which are repeated at regular intervals (abbreviated "Oc"), a group (Oc (3)) or a composite group (Oc (2+1)).

Isophase light - An isophase light, abbreviated "Iso", is a light which has dark and light periods of equal length. The prefix derives from the Greek *iso-* meaning "same".

Quick light - A quick light, abbreviated "Q", is a special case of a flashing light with a large frequency (more than 30 or 50 per minute). If the sequence of flashes is interrupted by regularly repeated eclipses of constant and long duration, the light is denoted "interrupted quick", abbreviated "I.Q".

Morse code - A Morse code light is light in which appearances of light of two clearly different durations (dots and dashes) are grouped to represent a character or characters in the Morse Code. For example, "Mo. (A)" is a light in which in each period light is shown for a short period (dot) followed by a long period (dash), the Morse Code for "A".

Fixed and flashing - A fixed and flashing light, abbreviated "F. Fl", is a light in which a fixed low intensity light is combined with a flashing high intensity light.

Alternating - An alternating light, abbreviate "Al", is a light which shows alternating colors. For example "Al WGB" show white, green and blue lights alternatively.

The USCG Light List is published in seven volumes and contains lights and other aids to navigation used for general navigation that are maintained by or under the authority of the U.S. Coast Guard and located in the waters surrounding the United States and its Territories.

Each volume corresponds to a different regional area and contains more complete information on each aid to navigation than can be conveniently shown on charts. This publication and the data contained within it is maintained and published by the USCG.

What Makes the Lighthouse's Light Flash?
The flashing light is produced by a round piece of glass called a bulls-eye lens that is very similar to the lens found in a magnifying glass.

The bulls-eye-lens is mounted in a large heavy optic called a Fresnel lens. This lens was invented by the French physicist Augustin-Jean Fresnel in the early 1800s. A Fresnel lens is made of many individual prisms that work

A Fresnel Lens concentrates and focuses light

together to focus light into a bright beam that can be seen from miles away. Most Fresnel lenses turn and produce a flash every time the bulls-eye lens passes in front of a light located in the center of the Fresnel lens assembly. The number of times a Fresnel lens appears to flash in a given amount of time produces a beacon's unique characteristic.

Before electricity, an elaborate clockwork mechanism turned the lens to create the individual flash characteristic. Much the way a grandfather's clock works today; slowly falling weights provided the propulsion to move the series of gears, which caused the lens to turn. The weights traveled down the center of the lighthouse tower. When the weights descended as far as they could go, the lighthouse keeper had to wind the clockwork mechanism to raise the weights and start the process over again. How often the keeper wound the clockwork depended upon how tall the lighthouse was and the lens's characteristic. Some lighthouses had to have the clockwork wound every few hours, all night long.

Lighthouse lens sizes

Fresnel produced six sizes of lighthouse lenses, divided into four *orders* based on their size and focal length. In modern use, these are classified as first through sixth order. An intermediate size between third and fourth order was added later, as well as sizes above first order and below sixth.

A first-order lens has a focal length of 36 in and an optical area 8.5 ft high. The complete assembly is about 12 ft tall and 6 ft wide. The smallest (sixth-order) has a focal length of 5.9 in and an optical area 17 in high.

Fresnel Light Order Descriptions

Order	# Wicks	Use
		First Order Fresnel Lens
1st	4	Largest Seacoast Lights.
2nd	3	Great Lakes Lighthouses, Seacoasts, Islands, Sounds.
3rd	2	Seacoasts, Sounds, River Entry, Bays, Channels, Range Lights.
4th	1	Shoals, Reefs, Harbor Lights, Islands in Rivers and Harbors.
5th	2	Breakwaters, River Lights, Channel, Small Islands in Sounds.
6th	1	Pier or Breakwater Lights in Harbors.

Lighthouse Markings

Lighthouses are most well known for alerting sailors to hazards and coastlines during the night, or through conditions that impede visibility, such as rain and fog. However, lighthouses also help to mark the coast by day.

A system developed by the Lighthouse Board *(est. 1852 by U.S. Congress)* designated individual lighthouses as "day marks" by the use of painted patterns. Unique patterns painted on lighthouses enable sailors to recognize them as markers for particular locations during the day. Although many lighthouses are painted with similar patterns, they are far enough apart to prevent them from being confused with one another.

Some lighthouses have simple bands of color, others are painted with spiraling lines and still others are painted one solid color. The most common colors used to paint lighthouses are white, black and red.

A few lighthouses notable for their markings include:

Bodie Island Light *(Nags Head, NC)*
Three white and two black horizontal bands

Cape Bonavista Light *(Bonavista, Newfoundland, Canada)* - white with vertical red

West Quoddy Head Light
(Lubec, ME) -
Eight thin, horizontal red stripes
against a white background

Cape Hatteras Light
(Outer Banks, NC)
Black spiral against a
white background

**Cape Lookout
Lighthouse** *(Cape Lookout
National Seashore, NC)* -
Large black and white
diamond pattern

Theodore Parker Burbank

Correctly match the Lighthouse/Fort with its apparition.

A Ghostly Quiz

Baker Island Light	Woman in Scarlet
Bird Island Lighthouse	Wife Who Has Only One Piece of Sheet Music
Minot's Ledge Lighthouse	Walled up Christmas Day duelist
Scituate Lighthouse	Captain Salty smokes pipe
Boston Light	Tunnels of Terror
Long Island Light	Three masted bark "Isadore"
Plymouth Lighthouse	The woman in White
Nauset Light	The Woman in Red
Nixes Mate	The Lady in Black
Nauset Light	The Guardian Ghost of "Little Sam"
Eastern Point Light	The Army of Two
Race Point Light	The "city slicker" second assistant keeper
New London Ledge Lighthouse	Teenage Boy and Rum Running Murderers
Stratford Shoal Light	Stored 400+ corpses in its freezer
Penfield Reef Lighthouse	Sailor's curse shrinks Light's Island into the sea
Boon Island Light	Replaces worn or storm tattered flags
Cape Neddick Light a/k/a Nubble Light	Red Hair Lady in Shawl Near Fireplace
Hendrick Head Lighthouse	Pirate's Lover became a witch and later swallowed by a whale
Marshall Point Light	Mysterious woman in seaweed
Matinicus Rock Lighthouse	Most Haunted Ship in the World
Mount Desert Rock Lighthouse	Lady in white waving a fiery torch

16

New England's Haunted Lighthouses and more

Owl's Head Lighthouse	Haunted by the ghost of an Indian Chief
Pemaquid Point Lighthouse	Guardian ghost of "Little Sam"
Portland Head Light	Ghosts of five murdered and one who committed suicide
Prospect Harbor Lighthouse	Ghosts of a mother and daughter and their German Sheppard dogs
Ram Island Lighthouse	Ghostly partiers knocking at the door
Sequin Island Lighthouse	Ghost the Screams "Keep Away" in Portuguese
West Quoddy Lighthouse	Ghost of the mother who's infant girl survived the sinking of the Helen and Mary
Winter Harbor Light	Ghost of pirate haunts outer Cape
Wood Island Light	Ghost of Keeper who's wife ran off w ferry captain
Portland Head Light	Ghost of Keeper Joshua Card
Portsmouth Harbor Lighthouse	Ghost of Custer's Ordnance Sergeant
Fort Constitution	Ghost of children obscure photos taken in the fort
Southeast Light, Block Island	Ghost of a Demon Dog
Harpswell, Maine	Ghost of "Mad Maggie"
New Haven, Connecticut	First Woman Lighthouse Keeper Still on the Job
Salem, Massachusetts	Drowned keeper still on duty
Block Island, Rhode Island	Dash – The "Ship of Death"
USS Constitution	Cursed founder speaks from his coffin - "Close the lid son"
Fort Strong	Classical Music Loving Ghost
Fort Warren	Chain Smoking Keeper's Wife
Fort Independence	Brass polishing ghost
Fort Knox	Baby that washed ashore and the "Woman in White"

Theodore Parker Burbank

Fort William Henry	Angry Keeper's ghost kept locked in the tower
Fort Wetherill	A Kissing Ghost
Fort Adams	"Palatine" a/k/a The Princess Augusta
USS Salem	"Noah's Dove"
Col Jonathan Buck Statue	"Great Shippe" in the Sky

Connecticut and Rhode Island

Haunted Lighthouses, Ships and Forts

Lighthouses:
New London Ledge Lighthouse
Penfield Reef Lighthouse
Southeast Light, Block Island
Stratford Shoals Light

Forts:
Fort Adams
Fort Wetherhill

Ships:
The Ghost Ship of New Haven
Ghost Ship *Palatine*

Shadow People

New London Ledge Lighthouse

Famous Ghost in Residence

Ernie, the Ghost of New London Ledge Lighthouse

The last entry in the Crew's Log before the light was automated was: *"Rock of slow torture. Ernie's domain. Hell on earth – may New London Ledge's light shine on forever because I'm through. I will watch it from afar while drinking a brew."* What was meaning behind the entry "Ernie's domain"? Who is or was Ernie and why was the station "Hell on Earth"? Facts about who Ernie was may be hard to confirm and hard to come by, but the many stories are not.

According to the most popular legend, Ernie was a keeper, probably in the 1920s or 30s. His younger and attractive wife, who lived ashore, is said to have run off with the Captain of the Block Island Ferry. Consumed with grief, anger and loneliness, Ernie is reported to have climbed to the roof of the lighthouse, slit his throat with his fishing knife and fell 65 feet into the Sound. His body was never recovered.

Legend has it that Ernie haunts and taunts those at the lighthouse to this day. He sometimes turns on the foghorn on clear days. There are cold spots inside, strange noises, whispers, boats are mysteriously untied, tools disappear and then reappear, furniture and other items are found rearranged, floors washed, windows cleaned, and that's not all.

Doors opening and closing themselves, unexplained knockings, bed sheets flying off of beds, cups moving on their own, TVs and radios turning on and off, items in locked desk drawers found rearranged, a fishy smell wafting through the rooms and other unexplained happenings. For example: the ghost of a tall, bearded man in a slicker and rain hat appears from time to time. Is this the ghost of Ernie?

In the 1990s, a Japanese television reporter spent a night at the lighthouse and recorded unexplainable loud whispering noises. Ledge Light and Ernie were featured the paranormal reality show *Scariest Places on Earth* and *Ghost Hunters*. Ernie has become a famous personality.

However, according to a visiting psychic in 1981, the ghost's name was revealed to be that of the former keeper John

Randolph, not someone named Ernie. Who then was Ernie and who was the first to give the apparition this name and why? We may never know the answers but one thing is certain; the lighthouse is haunted.

Unique Architectural Style
Since November 10, 1909 New London Ledge Lighthouse has sat upon its manmade island in Fishers Island Sound, at the mouth of the Thames River signaling the safe passage into New London Harbor. In 1906 congress appropriated $115,000 for its construction. A crew of four manned it until it was automated in 1987.

The lighthouse's original fourth-order Fresnel lens, made in France, is on display at the Custom House in New London. The characteristic of the beacon was three white flashes followed by a red flash every thirty seconds.

The unique three-story, eleven room brick and granite design of the structure was influenced by Edward Harkness and Morton Plant, prominent residents of Waterford and Groton, who wanted the lighthouse to resemble the styles of their homes and those of their neighbors. The result: architects developed a design incorporating both the Colonial Revival and French Second Empire styles of the Harkness and Plant mansions.

The Lighthouse Has a New Owner and Purpose

On May 1, 2013, the General Services Administration announced that New London Ledge Lighthouse was excess to the needs of the Coast Guard and was "being made available at no cost to eligible entities defined as federal agencies, state and local agencies, non-profit corporations, educational agencies, or community development organizations, for education, park, recreation, cultural, or historic preservation purposes." Interested entities were given sixty days to submit a letter of interest, and in 2014,the New London Maritime Society was announced as the new owner of the lighthouse. The New London Ledge Lighthouse Foundation will continue its use of the lighthouse.

Today the lighthouse serves as a maritime classroom, and plans are to open the lighthouse as a museum and perhaps provide overnight accommodations. Can you imagine the ad; "Spend the Night with a Mischievous Ghost – No Way Out until Dawn."

Station Stats
Station Established and First Lit: 1909
Deactivated: 1987
Foundation Materials: Concrete Pier
Construction Materials: Granite/Brick
Tower Shape: Cylindrical Tower on Dwelling
Markings/Pattern: Red w White Trim
Lens: Fourth Order, Fresnel
Characteristic: Three white flashes followed by a red flash every thirty seconds.

Animal Ghosts

Penfield Reef Lighthouse

Drowned Keeper Still on Duty

The light was constructed in 1874 at the end of mile-long Penfield Reef at a cost of $55,000. The reef has been referred to as "the most dangerous locality on Long Island Sound." It sits just over a mile off Fairfield Beach near Fairfield and Bridgeport, Connecticut.

Haunted by former Keeper

On December 22, 1916. Keeper Frederick A. Jordan launched the station's dory into a rough sea and headed for the mainland. He was off to join his family for the Christmas. He had not gone more than one hundred and fifty yards when his dory was capsized by a rouge wave. Assistant Keeper Rudolph Iten, fearful of launching the remaining dory into the violent wind and waves could only stand and watch Keeper Jordan being washed out to sea by the swift out going tide until he could be seen no more. The Assistant Keeper is quoted later, *"I will pass over the futile attempts I made to rescue him beyond telling you that it was a dirty day for weather and a nasty sea was running."*

Jordan's body was recovered and Assistant Keeper Iten was promoted to Keeper filling the shoes of the now deceased Keeper Jordan. Some nights later, during a storm that sent crashing waves over the top of the lighthouse, Keeper Iten was awakened *"by a strange feeling that someone was in my room."* Sitting up, Iten saw *"a gray, phosphorescent covered figure emerging from the room formerly occupied by Fred Jordan. It hovered at the top of the stairs, and then disappeared in the darkness below."* Later, when Iten went downstairs he found the station's logbook mysteriously moved to a table opened to the entry for December 22, 1916 — the night of Keeper Fred Jordan's drowning.

A newspaper article later quoted Keeper Iten: *"I have seen the semblance of the figure several times... and so have the others [two assistant keepers], and we are all prepared to take an affidavit to that effect. Something comes here, that we are positive. There is an old saying, 'What the Reef takes, the Reef will give back.'"*

More Ghostly Sightings and Strange Occurrences

For decades after the tragedy, keepers at the lighthouse reported the light behaving strangely for no apparent reason. In 1972 it was reported that the light was *"not flashing at maximum intensity and was monitored as flashing erratically."* This problem was attributed to the light's flasher. To this day mariners off the Connecticut coast claim that, in stormy weather, the spectre of a lighthouse keeper is seen on the lantern room gallery or floating above the reef itself. One owner of a power yacht reported that in rough weather his boat was guided to safety by a mysterious figure in a rowboat who vanished once the yacht reached safety.

On another occasion two boys who were fishing near the lighthouse were in danger of drowning after their boat capsized. A man seemingly appeared from nowhere and pulled the boys to safety on the rocks by the lighthouse. As the boys came to they entered the building expecting to find the keeper who had saved them, but there was nobody in sight. Whatever the explanation for these events, the legend of the ghost of Penfield Reef rivals that of Long Island Sound's other famous ghost, "Ernie" at New London Ledge Light.

William Hardwick, who became keeper in 1932, was born in Yorkshire, England and came to America as a boy. He spent a decade at sea followed by 23 years in the Lighthouse Service. While at Bridgeport Harbor Light, Hardwick saved the lives of seven crewmen on the Calvin Tompkins. He was at Penfield Reef in December 1935 when a fierce blizzard drove a Japanese steamer against the rocks, one of hundreds of vessels wrecked in the vicinity during the terrible storm.

He was still keeper on September 21, 1938, when the worst hurricane in Long Island Sound's recorded history struck.

Keeper Hardwick was on his way to the lighthouse in his 12-foot skiff when the great storm hit, and he soon realized that attempting to reach the station was fruitless. He made it back to the mainland where he spent the night, while an assistant weathered the storm at Penfield Reef. Three years later William Hardwick decided he had enough of lighthouse keeping. He rowed through heavy seas to Fairfield Beach and reached his wife at their onshore home, and told her simply, "Millie, I'm through with that job."

Penfield Reef Light has also had the distinction of having two women serve as assistant keepers — assistants Pauline Jones and June Martin, who were both married to keepers. After nearly a century of resident keepers, Penfield Reef Light was automated in 1971.

Excerpted from the October 2002 edition of Lighthouse Digest Magazine

Station Stats
Construction material: Granite, wood
Height of tower: 35 feet
Height of focal plane: 51 feet
Original optic: Fourth-order Fresnel lens
Present optic: VRB-25 (solar powered)
Characteristic: Flashing red every six seconds (active U.S. Coast Guard aid to navigation)
Fog signal: One blast every 15 seconds

Demon Ghosts

Southeast Light, Block Island

The Ghost of "Mad Maggie"

Block Island is a twenty-five square mile island that is six miles long laying fifteen miles east of Long Island Sound. It lays midway between Montauk Point Light and the lighthouse at Point Judith, RI and is an essential navigational aid for shipping between New York and the North East. Many ships have run afoul on the submerged rocks and sandy shoals surrounding the island, often called the "stumbling block" of the New England coast.

The lighthouse sits two hundred feet atop Mohegan Bluff, a sandy, clay cliff that is continually being eroded away. In 1993 the 2,000-ton structure was moved back away from the cliff nearly two hundred yards.

The original Block Island Light was washed out to sea during a violent storm and in 1856, congress appropriated $9,000 to construct its replacement. The brick Gothic Revival style structure was completed in 1875.

The tower is 67 feet in height, with an octagonal granite foundation. A sixteen-sided pyramidal copper roof tops brick exterior with a ball ventilator and lightning rod. The original roof was cast iron, and replaced in 1994. The attached 2-½-story keeper's house has two wings. The north wing housed the keeper, and the south wing his assistants.

The original optic was a first order 12-foot tall Fresnel lens with its four circular wicks, fueled by whale oil and is on display in the lighthouse's gift shop. The wicks consumed an average of nine hundred gallons of whale oil a year. The whale oil was replaced by kerosene in 1880 and the lens modified to rotate floating in a pool of mercury, driven by a clock whose weights had to be rewound every four hours.

Mad Maggie, the Ghost Who Hates Men

In the early 1900's the keeper of Block Island's Southeast Light, despite his protestations that it was suicide, was convicted of murdering his wife by throwing her down the tower's stairs.

It was common knowledge that Maggie was consistently angry and constantly nagging and berating her husband. All that knew her called her "Mad Maggie". Other than her apparent unhappiness with "her man" she was thought to be reasonably content with her lot. Therefore, the jury discarded the theory that she had committed suicide and instead found for the prosecution. It was far easier to believe that the keeper, possibly in a furious rage, pushed his nagging wife down the tower stairs.

Her husband went to jail but she remains on the island harassing subsequent keepers and men in general. Women and children apparently are immune to her wrath and anger. She apparently is still angry, as many have heard her banging pots and pans in the kitchen and dashing furniture about in the rest of the house.

She appears to take pleasure in tormenting men. Some of her nasty tricks included; tossing men out of their bed by lifting the bed off the floor and shaking it, locking men in their room or in closets. She once frightened a keeper out of his bed and chased him out into the cold night locking the doors behind him. He was wearing only his underwear.

The telephone was located inside the dwelling as was his key. The only other key was at the Coast Guard station on the other side of the island. How embarrassing it must have been for him not only to have walk barefooted across the island but to arrive wearing only his undies.

In 1993, Mad Maggie was apparently very unhappy about the lighthouse and dwelling being moved back away from the eroding cliff. Workmen reported her throwing food at them if they tried to eat in her kitchen. She constantly was rearranging the furniture and heard running up and down the tower stairs in a rage.

Chrissy's Gang

Ship-wreckers, or "Mooncussers" was the way entire communities supported themselves. One could say they were really land-based pirates. They would light fires along the treacherous cliffs, luring

unsuspecti ng ships onto the sands and rocks and their demise. Their deception would only work on

moonless nights and therefore "Cuss the moon" that kept them from their devious work.

In the early eighteenth century, the "wreckers" rescued a shipwrecked Dutch woman named Chrissy. She would build a shack right where she landed and make her living the same way those that had rescued her did. She would wade out deep into the water, carrying a club with which she would dispatch any survivors from the ships. She was so good at luring in ships, and collecting the flotsam, that she had a following, known as Chrissy's Gang.

Her ruthlessness was legendary, and became even more so when one day she encountered a man floating in the water that she recognized. It was her son Edward, who'd given up the lawless life and went to sea as a merchant sailor many years before. He looked up and said, "It's me, mom." She looked him dead in the eye and clubbed him to death. Her reasoning? " A son is but a son, but a wreck is survival."

Minister - Either Become a Mooncusser or Starve

In the 1600's, at Block Island, a minister came out to the island from the mainland to try to stop the wreckers. Preacher Seth Baldwin was unable to stop the murderous thievery, and the islanders would not support him monetarily. Soon, Preacher Baldwin was starving, and asked that each island family donate some food to him, even just a potato. The request was not unusual as this was the customary way communities supported their clergy in tough monetary times..

The islanders denied the request, but came to their own solution to prevent the man of God and his family from starving. They voted to give him his very own hook (which was a pole with a bent nail in it to hook into the flotsam), and make it one inch longer than the rest so he would have a little advantage. They felt if he couldn't support himself with that edge, then he deserved to starve to death. How this ended is not known.

Phantom Pirate Ships and Spirits Waiting to be Buried

Many people have reported sighting a phantom pirate ships sailing off the lighthouse cliff. Also, the spirits of souls who died midwinter are seen eternally wandering about waiting for the ground to thaw, so they can be buried. They have been spotted wandering all around the island.

Station Stats

Year constructed: 1875 - Lit: 1875
Automated: 1990, - Deactivated: 1990-1994
Construction: Red brick
Tower shape: Octagonal pyramidal tower attached to dwelling
Height: 52 feet - Range: 20 Nautical miles
Original lens: 1st order Fresnel lens (1875)
Current lens: 1st order Fresnel lens from Cape Lookout Light

Stratford Shoals Light

Ghost of the Suicidal Assistant

Dutch explorer Adriaen Block's (he gave Block Island its name) 1614 map of the sound show two small islands where the Lighthouse now stands, and which have since been washed away, named Middleground.

Is it in New England or New York?

It was the state of New York, not Connecticut, which in 1874 ceded the shallow mile wide shoal located in the middle of Long Island Sound to the federal government. The Light is alternatively called Middleground or Middle Ground Light because it is essentially in the middle of the 11.3-mile wide Sound. However, modern measuring methods place the light on the Connecticut side by 1,000 feet.

In 1873 Congress appropriated $10,000 for a "floating light for Middle Ground, Long Island Sound". The lightship referred to as LV15, was 73 feet long and weighed 100 tons. It was dragged from its station by ice several times, most notably in 1875 when it ran aground at Orient Point, and again in 1876 when it drifted to Faulkner Island. In 1877 $125,000 was appropriated for the construction of the Stratford Shoal lighthouse as the replacement of the lightship LV15.

A foundation was constructed in the shallow reefs waters, only two feet deep at low tide, and the granite pier surrounded by thirty tons of granite rip rap to protect the foundation from the waves and strong Long Island Sound currents from undermining the structure.

In December 1877 the 35-foot gray granite, gable-roofed lighthouse became operational, with a fourth-order Fresnel lens exhibiting a flashing white light every ten seconds 60 feet above sea level. The station being several miles from shore and no land of its own for one to stretch his legs provided for the most difficult and isolated condition for its Keeper and his two assistants.

The *Bridgeport Sunday Post* described life at the Shoal in 1927:

Through the turmoil and the windswept spume, people on shore see the light gleaming in intermittent flashes from Middle Ground scarcely realizing that out there in all that fury of element and tumbling water, a handful of men are keeping watch and ward over that dreary waste and insuring a safe passage for the country's shipping

One-Week Alone With a Madman
In 1905, Julius Koster, a rookie Second Assistant keeper from

New York and First Assistant Morrell Hulse a fifty-four-year-old Long Island native where left alone on the Light while the Head Keeper Gilbert Rulon was ashore.

According to contemporaneous newspaper reports, Julius attacked Morrell with a straight razor lashed to the end of a pole. Fortunately, Morrell was able to quell the attack and calm his attacker down.

Julius continued to threaten Morrell in various ways causing him to fear for his life. Five days later, the troubled Julius locked himself into the lantern room with an axe, jammed the rotation of the light and threatened to smash it and kill himself. Again, Morrell was able to persuade Julius to put down the axe and come down from the tower. Julius put the axe down and instead of coming down he threw himself off the tower into the cold water of the Sound.

Morrell was able to pull him from the water back into the lighthouse saving his life. Morrell had been unable to sleep since the first

incident so, in order to protect himself and get some much-needed rest; he tied Julius up for the two days it took for help to arrive.

Julius was transported to New York, where a few days later he did succeed in taking his life. Although he didn't die at the light, his spirit appears to have returned with a vengeance. Doors slam shut in the middle of the night, chairs are thrown against the walls, posters have been ripped down and hot pans of water have been flung from the stove. The lighthouse was automated in 1969, and the last of the Coast Guard personnel left, probably with no regrets. To this day, however, sailors passing close by can still hear thumps, bumps, grinding noises and loud sounds as Julius continues to throw tantrums.

Was it the Light's isolation and *"Dreary Waste"* as the Bridgeport Sunday Post reported that drove Second Assistant Keeper Julius Koster mad? Was it the sudden extreme contrast between the hustle and bustle of his native New York City and the loneliness and boredom of life and routine at Stratford Shoals Lighthouse? Why did his ghost return to haunt this lonely light?

Theodore Parker Burbank

Station Stats
Station Established: 1837
Year Current Tower(s) First Lit: 1877
Deactivated: 1970
Foundation Materials: Granite Ashlar Caisson
Construction Materials: Granite Blocks
Tower Shape: Octagonal Tower on Square Dwelling
Markings/Pattern: Natural with White Lantern
Original Lens: Fourth Order Fresnel

Fort Adams

Tunnels of Terror

Fort Adams, Newport, RI – established July 4th, 1799

Small wonder that this fort is haunted. Since its establishment in 1779 it has been the site of many tragic and untimely deaths. Unfortunately, many construction workers were killed during the construction of the fort, sort of setting the stage for what was to come.

Exactly twenty years after the establishment of the fort, on July 4th, 1819, one private William Cornell shot a fellow soldier at point blank range, killing him instantly. There were no known issues between the two men however, as the fort was celebrating the nation's independence, an extra ration of rum had been allocated to the troops. Was Demon Rum at the root of the problem?

The Spanish Flu outbreak of 1918 claimed sixty-two lives at the fort. Especially tragic is the case of Delia Theresa Geary, a pregnant, 25-year-old wife of Irish immigrant and U.S. Army Lt. Richard Geary. Both had contracted the flu and she delivered a baby girl prematurely. The lives of Lt. Geary, his wife and newborn child were claimed by the flu.

Then on January 25, 1925, the frozen and snow covered body of Mary Gleason, also an Irish immigrant, was found at the bottom of an Artillery ditch at the fort. Mary came to the fort to be with Private George Henderson with whom she had "been keeping company." She brought a basket filled with sandwiches, cookies and small cakes. No one is sure what exactly transpired. Some say she lost her footing and fell 31 feet off the wall into the ditch where she lay for three days before her frozen corpse was found. Others claim her death a murder involving a love triangle.

Today those touring the fort report hearing heavy metal doors slamming shut and footsteps on wooden floors that had long ago rotted away. Others say the have seen the shapes of shadowy people out of the corner of their eyes and a voice commanding, "Go away." The shadow of a man, perhaps a soldier, pacing back and forth atop the ramparts is a frequent visitor. Physical interaction between visitors and those entities on "the Other Side" include being pushed, women being grouped and faces slapped by an unseen protagonist.

Tunnels of terror

History

Fort Adams was established on July 4 1799 as a coastal fortification. The fort is named in honor of President John Adams. Maj Louis de Tousard of the Army Corps of Engineers designed the first fort. The fort mounted 12 cannons and was armed during the War of 1812. After the War of 1812, there was a thorough review of the nation's fortification needs and it was decided to replace the older fort with a newer, larger fort.

Brigadier General Simon Bernard, who had served as a military engineer under Napoleon, designed the new fort. Construction began in 1824 and continued until 1857. The new fort was first armed in August 1841, functioning as an active Army post until 1950. During this time the fort was active in five major wars (the Mexican-American War, American Civil War, Spanish-American, World War I and World War II) but never fired a shot. During the Mexican-American War the fort was briefly under the command of Brigadier General Franklin Pierce who later was elected President of the United States in 1852.

In 1861 The US Naval Academy was moved to Fort Adams from Annapolis Maryland. In Sept 1861 the Naval Academy moved to the Atlantic House Hotel in Newport and remained there until the end of the Civil War.

In 1953 the US Army gave the fort to the US Navy. In 1965 the fort was given to the State of Rhode Island for use as Fort Adams State Park. The eighty-acre Fort Adams State Park was declared a National Historical Landmark in 1976.

Tour the Fort

The Fort Adams Trust provides an hour long guided tour that takes you from the top of the Fort walls to the depths of the underground listening tunnels. Daily tours depart hourly 10am-4pm.

Reported to be the Ghosts of an Irish bride and groom

The Trust comments: *"The soldiers and military officers that once called Fort Adams home may be gone, but the paranormal energy they left behind still incites shivers in Fortress of Nightmares visitors.*

Guests confront the supernatural through several routes, one being ghost hunts. These 90-minute excursions into the unknown call upon The Rhode Island Paranormal Research group and knowledgeable tour guides to escort patrons through the facilities, answering questions about the barracks, officers' quarters, casemates, and slabs of haunted meatloaf in the mess hall.

Theodore Parker Burbank

Adventurers get even closer to lingering entities through rental electro-magnetic field detectors and infrared thermometers. Horror also reigns in the Tunnels of Terror, possessed stretches shrouded in spooky light and sound effects, and the zombie-themed Apocalypse airsoft range. Ghost tours offer a less-frightening look into the fort's history and stories, thanks to a local-folklore expert who accompanies the tour guide."

Fort Wetherhill State Park

Ghost of a Demon Black Dog

Fort Wetherhill atop 100 ft cliffs

Fort Wetherill State Park, on the Island of Conanicut (Jamestown), sits high upon 100-foot high granite cliffs across the water from Fort Adams State. The Parks 61.5 acres were formally acquired by the State of Rhode Island from the United States in 1972.

The Ghost of the Phantom Black Dog

A phantom Black Dog has been menacing this fort since 1776 when the British, after taking over the fort, reported being terrorized by a large black dog with glaring red eyes and huge snarling fangs.

There are no reports he has harmed anyone, although, those who have seen him are usually never quite the same. Some visitors have sworn they have felt a chilling breath, perhaps the Dog's, on the backs of their necks. Others report hearing the Black Dog's eerie howls rise above the winds sending a terrifying chill through their bodies. There is no reason to worry about an encounter with the Black Dog as the Black Dog is said to be harmless; as long as he is left alone.

What made the British soldier even more terrified by this apparition was that, in British folklore of the time, a black dog symbolized death. According to the legend, the Black Dog is a harbinger of death, and those who are unfortunate enough to encounter the spirit are fated to die or meet with great misfortune within a year's time. Looking into the Black Dog's fiery eyes means certain death within a year.

The Black Dog is described as being huge with shaggy fur as black as the night and larger than most dogs. The Black Dog's most frightening features are his glowing, fiery red eyes.

Phantom Black Dog haunts the Fort

The phantom dog continues to present itself to the unwary, its fearsome eyes ablaze; often walking through the solid walls of the fort. Its barking and howling is often heard coming from within the empty chambers of the fort.

The Fort's History

In the 18th Century, a crude earthwork fortification was constructed at the site of Dumpling Rock, which overlooks the strategic East Passage toward Newport, to prevent British attacks on Newport at the outbreak of the Revolution. The British attacked and captured the unfinished fortification on in December 1776. During the Revolutionary War American, British and French forces occupied the fort for various periods of time. The British abandoned the fort at Dumpling Rock on October 25, 1779 when they evacuated Newport.

In 1798 the Army Corps of Engineers began construction of a permanent fortification at Dumpling Rock. This fort was originally named Fort Louis and later changed to Fort Brown (after Major General Jacob Brown commanding general of the United States Army

In 1899 the United States Government expanded the fort and renamed it Fort Wetherill for Captain Alexander M. Wetherill who died at San Juan Hill in Cuba.

Ghostly Family

The Ghost Ship of New Haven

"Great Shippe" in the Sky

Ghost ship in the sky

In 1702 the Reverend Cotton Mather wrote in his book "Magalia Christi Americana" of the attempts in 1647 of the colonies to establish "remunerative commerce" in New Haven. A group of prominent citizens commissioned the building of a *"Great Shippe"* at a shipyard in Rhodes Island.

The ship would be the catalyst to build wealth in the fledgling settlement through trade with England and Europe. Merchandise of every stripe would be assembled from all over Connecticut and carried abroad upon this grand vessel.

The ship was completed and brought to New Haven Harbor to be loaded with goods for its maiden voyage. Things did not start well. The winter had been exceptionally cold therefore, in order to exit the Harbor; ice had frozen blocking the harbor and had to be cleared by hand in order to get the ship into Long Island sound.

The Reverend John Davenport uttered these prophetic words in prayer at the inauspicious launching: *"Lord, if it be thy pleasure to bury these our Friends in the bottom of the Sea, they are thine; save them!"* With this unusual "Benediction" the ship slipped away into a thick fog, never to be seen again.

Months passed; ships left and returned from Europe and not a one was able to report on the whereabouts of the *Great Shippe*. Nearly a year and a half passed when a particularly wild summer thunderstorm hit New Haven harbor. In its immediate aftermath spectators claimed to have seen a vivid phantom version of the *Great Shippe* sailing in the sky, its masts battered and its sails torn.

Ghost Ship *Palatine* a/k/a *The Princess Augusta*

Sailing for Eternity off Block Island

Late in 1752, two hundred forty German immigrants and a crew of fourteen-left Holland anticipating a new life in America's new city of Philadelphia. Their arduous journey would culminate in mutiny, piracy, terrible sickness and death. The ill-fated journey would end in a fiery crash on a beach on the southern tip of Block Island, Rhode Island.

The crossing of the Atlantic in mid winter proved to be disastrous. Constant storms and heavy seas battered the aging ship. The ship was slowly falling apart in the constant storms and the food had spoiled. Two hundred of the passengers and seven of the crew died of "fever and flux" because of a contaminated water supply and spoiled food.

Mutiny Aboard the Palatine
Finally, on December 27 in a New England "nor'easter", the ship was within sight of land off of Block Island. Captain George Long, dropped anchor while several miles off shore in an attempt to ride out the gale. However, the crew in rebellion to the

captain's decision decided to mutiny, take charge of the ship and head towards land and the safety they believed the signal lights on the beach represented.

They murdered the captain, and then the mutineers became pirate and robbed the surviving passengers of their valuables, killing any who resisted and headed the ship towards the signal lights and rockets thinking they were headed towards safety and safe haven from the storm.

Mutineers Fall For a Trap

The signal lights on the shore and the rockets that lit the sky were part of a trap of the "Mooncussers." Mooncussers were land-based pirates who, on dark moonless nights, would erect a decoy signal fire, and then, after having caused a shipwreck, subdue or often kill, any survivors and plunder the wreckage for valuables

It was a trap that the mutineers fell for lock, stock and barrel. As the ship came closer to the shore, one of the signal rockets landed on board the Palatine setting it ablaze.

Because of the heavy gale winds the small fire became an inferno almost

Ship ablaze after hit by **signal rocket**

immediately. Screams of terror could clearly be heard above the sounds of the wind and surf. Many jumped to their death in the surf rather than be burned alive. Finally, the ship was driven up upon the rocks and broke to pieces almost immediately.

Witch on Board Curses the Island

There were few survivors; one of note was "Dutch" Kattern who claimed she was a witch. It is said she put a curse on Block Island stating that the islanders would; *"suffer the sight of the Palatine in flames off its shores, rather than the idyllic view of the ocean."*

To this day, many claim to see a bizarre orange light off the shore of Sandy Point. It is said to resemble a ship on fire, slowly sailing off Sandy Point. Some say this a curse brought about by the evil deeds the mutinous crew carried out long ago. Others believe that this is the ghost of the *Palatine* returning to haunt those who set her ablaze with their rockets long ago.

Many people walking along the shore near the marker that marks the mass grave of victims who washed ashore report hearing muted cries for help coming from the sea. Are these the cries of the spirits of those who drowned here so many years ago?

Famous Poet Memorializes the Event

The poet John Greenleaf Whittier in a poem named *The Palatine*, which faithfully adapts the traditional story in verse, immortalized the legend. Whittier heard the tale in 1865 from Newport resident Joseph P. Hazard, whose family were key informants for collectors of 19th-century New England folklore. It was printed in the *Atlantic Monthly* in 1867 and later appeared in his collection *The Tent on the Beach* later that year, and became one of his best known works. The popularity of the *Palatine* name is largely due to Whittier's poem.

John Greenleaf Whittier

John Greenleaf Whittier, born in Haverhill, Massachusetts, on December 17, 1807, was an influential American Quaker poet and ardent advocate of the abolition of slavery in the United States.

Burning Ship Still Being Spotted

On the Saturday between Christmas and New Year's Eve there are still sporadic reports from the locals of seeing a burning ship sail past. Tradition states that on December 26, 1738, a German ship carrying immigrants to Philadelphia, ran aground during a snowstorm and was stranded near Block Island. Depositions from the remaining crewmembers reported a loss of half the crew.

Two Versions of the Legend

However, folklorist Michael Bell while investigating the legend noted that two versions of the tragic event began to be circulated almost a year after the incident.

Block Islanders insisted that their citizens had made a valiant effort to rescue the crew, whilst those on the mainland of New England suspected the islanders of luring the ship towards them in an effort to seize their cargo. Both legends agreed that a female passenger had refused to leave the ship as it sank, and those who claim to witness its reappearances say that her screams are heard from the ship. Today a marker exists on the spot where the ship is thought to have run aground, by

Marker of *Palatine* victims mass grave

the Mohegan Bluffs, which reads: *Palatine Graves - 1738.*

Those who believe in the legend claim that those who died that night lay buried under the soil. However, Charlotte Taylor of the Rhode Island Historical Preservation and Heritage Commission has noted that no physical evidence has ever been found to substantiate that claim, nor the legend itself.

Block Island lies directly within the very busy shipping lane between New York and Boston; ideally situated for those determined to lure ships onto its rocky shores. Perhaps that is why the island gained a reputation, perhaps undeservedly, as a haven of "wreckers" or "moon cursers." These nefarious scoundrels would light false beacons to encourage wrecks, and even kill the survivors, though the veracity of such stories is debatable.

Theodore Parker Burbank

Angel Ghost

Massachusett's Haunted Lighthouses, Ships and Forts

North Shore
Bakers Island Light
Bird Island Light
Eastern Point Light
Ghost Ship of Salem

Boston Harbor
Boston Light
Nixes Mate Island Beacon
Long Island Light - Fort Strong
USS Constitution
USS Salem – 139
Castle Island
Fort Warren

South Shore
Cohasset Lighthouse
Minot Light
Plymouth Lighthouse - Brown's Bank
Scituate Light - Cohasset Shipwrecks
Plymouth Lighthouse -

Cape Cod
Nauset Light
Race Point Light

Demon Ghost

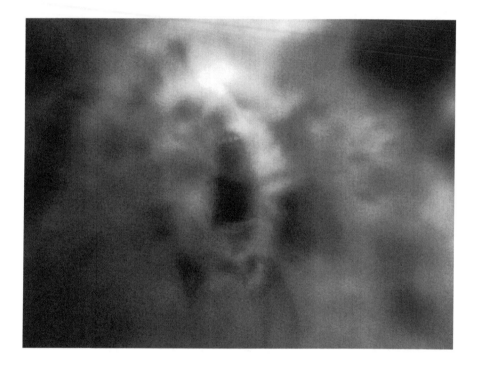

Baker's Island Lighthouse

Numerous Ghosts Haunts the Light

US Coast Guard Photo Circa 1925

The station was originally established in 1791, with a day mark. This was replaced in 1798 by two lights atop a keeper's house, one at each end. After storm damage in 1815, an octagonal stone tower was constructed. The current round stone tower was added in 1820. The 1820 tower was taller, leading to the names "Ma" and "Pa". The two remained in service until 1926, when the older, shorter tower was removed.

Baker's Island is one of a group of 15 islands called the Miseries, lying some five miles out from Salem Harbor. Consisting of 55 acres and dotted with rambling old summerhouses with wide porches, the island serves as a seasonal retreat for a select group of New Englanders—mostly from the Salem area. In addition to the houses, there is also a general store, pump house and, of course, the Bird Island Lighthouse.

Meet the Ghosts
There are several ghosts that, for more than one hundred years, are reported to haunt the island.

Horn Blowing Ghost - Perhaps the most annoying ghost haunting the island is the poltergeist that delights in interrupting the sleep of keepers and caretakers by activating the lighthouse's foghorn. Caretakers report the foghorn sounding "for no reason on crystal clear nights." Strangely, the foghorn sounds only on nights that are clear and not during storms. Some theorize this ghost to be a hapless sailor who, during a foggy night, perhaps more than one hundred years ago, was shipwrecked and drowned off the island.

In 1898 several of the former lighthouse keepers held a reunion on the island. That night, as they were departing on the ferry, they all heard the foghorn sounding loudly. During the return to the mainland a violent storm hit and their ferry capsized. All but one of the light keepers drowned. Was the horn sounding a warning?

Kissing Ghost - Workers at the Wells Cottage report having been attacked by a "kissing ghost." Specific details of the occurrences remain unreported and therefore are not available.

Partying Ghost(s) - Caretakers have reported hearing what they say sounds like a party coming from the Chase Cottage even though it is closed up tight for the winter. Family members have reportedly seen filmy shapes darting about the halls, and at least one member claims to have encountered an evil presence in the house.

Ghostly Shopper - Lights are sometimes seen in the general store when the store is closed for the season.

The Light Flicking Ghost – Scores of people have reported seeing lights flickering on and off in several of the cottages during the winter when the buildings are unoccupied. There is no electricity on the island save for solar panels and generators yet the lights flicker nonetheless.

The Haunted Fog Horn –**Repeatedly Struck by Lightning**
Prior to the fog siren installed in 1906, a loud fog bell, operated by an automatic, clockwork type mechanism, sounded the alarm for mariners. The fog bell ran perfectly only one time, but then it was struck by lightning in 1877 and never ran correctly again.

The bell was replaced, but even the new one kept failing, and would not work. When the fog bell didn't work, the light keeper or his assistant had to go out and strike the bell manually with a hammer at the prescribed interval, so the sailors wouldn't go aground on the rocks.

In 1879, the bell tower was again struck by lightning, and was demolished. But the new, third one didn't work either, and finally keeper Rogers left the post in frustration. Records are spotty after he left, but seventeen years later he returned for a visit. When he and the others on the steamer left the island, the fog bell started up inexplicably.

After dropping a few persons off at a harbor, a waterspout appeared and lifted the boat out of the water and turned it upside down, drowning all but a few on board. The former keeper was one of those that survived, and some think the bell may have been trying to warn him.

Later that day, the fog bell was once again struck by lightning, and destroyed. Even to this day, the foghorn goes off unpredictably, even when the night is clear and cold.

Station Stats
Station established: 1791 – Current lighthouse tower built: 1820 - Automated: 1972 Construction material: Granite - Tower height: 59 feet - Height of focal plane: 111 feet Previous optic: Fourth order Fresnel lens (1855) Present optic: VRB-25 Light Characteristic: Alternating white and red flashes every 20 seconds Fog signal: One three-second blast every 30 seconds

Bird Island Lighthouse –

The Pirate Who Became a Lighthouse Keeper

Bird Island is situated merely yards off Butler's Point near the head of Buzzards Bay at the entrance to Sippican Harbor. It takes its name from the endangered Roseate Terns that nest there. The 1.5-acre island is the habitat for nearly one-third of this endangered species

Charles Bradley, founder of the Bird Island Lighthouse Preservation Society, states that Bird Island is one of the nation's oldest original lighthouse structures. Other lighthouse may be older, but their structures have been replaced or rebuilt. Congress appropriated funds for the lighthouse in March of 1819 and it was activated later that year on September 1.

Pirate was the First Keeper

William S. Moore, an alleged pirate and veteran of the War of 1812, was appointed the first Keeper at Bird Island Lighthouse in 1819.

It is said that Moore's wife, a fading beauty and "Boston Society Girl", had tuberculosis and was a very heavy smoker. Mainlanders are reported to have secretly smuggled bags of tobacco to her in order to in order to satisfy her addiction and muffle her moanful cries for the substance.

Wife Murdered

Moore is claimed to have murdered his wife and hid her body somewhere on the small island and then disappear. Another version says that he killed his wife in an argument caused by his refusing to take her to the mainland for medical treatment and tobacco. It is said he was afraid she would leave him now that his pirating fortunes were diminished.

Another story is that after his wife's death Moore raised the distress flag attracting the minister who bravely made his way across the ice to the island. He performed a burial ceremony for her and then helped Moore dig her grave.

Moore is said to have blamed his wife's death on the villagers who provided her with tobacco. He in turn was blamed for her death for not allowing her off the island to obtain medical treatment. Although there was no evidence to support the theory, many suspected Moore of murdering his wife during one of their many heated arguments. Although she is reportedly buried on the island, there is no evidence of the grave anywhere to be found.

Ghost of a Woman Scares Away the Next Keeper

It is reported that Moore's replacement fled the light in terror upon seeing the ghost of a woman, never to return after spending only a couple of nights at the light. Ever since, the island has been called cursed and haunted and reports of ghostly sightings abound. "The ghost of a hunched-over old woman, rapping at the door during the night", reportedly frightened later keepers.

Island Called Cursed

Peter Murray, keeper in 1891, believed the island was cursed. One especially severe winter, his eleven-month-old son was struck with pneumonia. Lacking the means to leave the island, Murray doused the tower light praying to attract attention. When help finally arrived, it was too late. The family buried the infant on the mainland. They never returned to haunted Bird Island.

Theodore Parker Burbank

Station Stats

Station established: 1819 –

Current lighthouse tower built: 1819

Deactivated 1933-1997 –

Relighted 1997

Height of focal plane: 37 feet

Earlier optic: Fourth order Fresnel lens (1856)

Present optic: 300 mm, solar powered,

White Flashes for 0.6 seconds every 6 seconds

Eastern Point Light
Sea Serpents, Famous Guest and Ghosts

This lighthouse marks the entrance to "America's oldest seaport", Gloucester Harbor. Fishermen, traders, smugglers and even pirates have been using the harbor since 1616. Records from 1830 through 1910 show 779 vessels and 5,305 seafarers "out of Gloucester," were lost at sea.

Eastern Point Light Tragedy
Secret, Gory, Winter Horror

It was an exceptionally cold winter with strong gale winds, unusual wet and heavy snow buffeting the lighthouse and its buildings on Eastern Point. Inside the keeper's houses were living a mother and daughter along with their two German shepherd dogs.

There are not too many people living in the mansions lining the road out to the Point during the winter and those who were there were not prone to be walking about in the kind of weather being inflicted upon them. Therefore, the lack of activity at the Keeper's dwelling that winter went entirely un-noticed by everyone. It was not until springtime that the gruesome scene and fate of two women and their pets was discovered.

Gruesome Discovery

Authorities, attempting entry into the dwelling, found the door blocked by something on the other side. They forced the door open and the grizzly scene began to unfold. The decomposing remains of what appeared to be a German Shepherd dog were blocking the door.

No one is perfectly clear as to just what happened but authorities and family surmise that the mother probably had taken ill during the deepest part of the bitter cold winter and took to her bed leaving her daughter to take care of her and their dogs.

The timing of events are unclear However, as women were found dead, the daughter in her rocking chair in front of the parlor stove and her elderly mother upstairs in her bed; it is thought the daughter became incapacitated or died leaving her frail mother to perish alone.

The Tragic Story Continues

The two dogs were now alone in the house, their masters both having died. The scratch marks on the doors indicate the dog's frantic attempts to get out of the house. They needed food and water and no one was there to feed them – or was there? One dog was found upstairs. He was lying on the bed next to the dismembered body of his caretaker. Her leg and arm bones scattered about the room.

Downstairs the scene was similar. The daughter was still mostly sitting in her rocker, the fire was out and her arm and leg bones also strewn about the room.

Can you imagine such a horrid scene? Can you imagine being the only relative (distant) left and the one responsible to clean up the site?

This tale was told the author by a surviving relative. No one on the point talks of the horror. Might knowledge of the horrific event effect property values?

Four Spirits Haunting the Light?

Eastern Point Lighthouse does not have many neighbors but it is said that, especially on winter nights, that sound of frantic scratching can be heard near the downstairs exit doors. Also reportedly heard, coming from the living room, is the sound of a chair rocking upon a wooden floor.

Do the ghosts of the hapless mother and daughter and their dogs haunt the lighthouse? Wait, do I hear a dog barking?

Sea Serpent

In 1638 John Josselyn, Gent - Maine's first natural history writer, recorded the first sighting of the monster, now known as the "Gloucester Sea Serpent." He was prevented from shooting it by his Indian companion who warned that terrible bad luck would befall him if he did.

THE SEA SERPENT

Multiple Sea Serpent Sightings

It was August 10, 1817 and reports of a Monstrous Sea Serpent filled the news of the day. General David Humphreys, formerly of George Washington's staff, came to Gloucester to determine the veracity of the

Honorable Lonso Nash, then a magistrate of the town of Gloucester, saw the sea-serpent in August 1817 in the Gloucester Harbor. Ten depositions were passed in to him all swearing as to the particulars. It was eighty or ninety feet long, had a body the size of a half barrel, a very dark color, and a tongue that resembled a harpoon two feet long. The serpent swam twelve or fourteen miles an hour. It never swam down into the water but rather sank down as a rock. It had eight distinct bunches or portions above water. An earlier one had been seen in 1639 on Cape Ann. The existence of such an animal had been vouched for by Pontopiddan, Bishop of Bergen, by Reverend Donald M'lean of Scotland, by a man in Plymouth, Mass. in 1815, by several persons in Long Island Sound in 1817, and some who saw him off of Nahant, Mass. the same year. Also a Reverend W. Cummings saw a sea monster in Penobscot Bay in 1809

reports. He interviewed scores of witnesses who reported, *"Its head was much like the head of a turtle... and larger than the head on any dog." From its head there rose "a prong or spear about twelve inches in height, and six inches in circumference at the bottom, and running to a small point."*

The *Boston Weekly Messenger* described the creature as sixty to seventy feet in length, about as wide as a barrel, moved rapidly in a serpentine fashion, was able to double back upon itself instantaneously, *"full of joints and resembled a string of buoys on a net,"* that all attempts to kill or capture it, including shooting a musket at it from close range, failed.

History
Built, Rebuilt and Built Again
Construction of the first lighthouse began in 1831 by adding a wrought iron lantern and copper dome to the existing day-marker. Conversion to a 30 ft lighthouse was completed and the white light lit on New Years Day 1832.

The lighthouse was rebuilt in 1848 with a 34 ft tower that showed a fixed red light locals called "Ruby Light." The cost to build the new lighthouse was $2,550. The light was activated on November 3, 1848.

The present 36 ft conical brick tower erected in 1890 upon the foundation of the demolished 1848 tower. The new brick tower was painted white with a black lantern and red roof. The light flashes white every five seconds and is visible for 20 nautical miles.

Breakwater and Beacon Constructed
The 2,250 foot long breakwater over the dangerous "Dog Bar Reef" was completed in 1905 at a cost of $300,000 using 231,756 tons of Cape Ann granite. Gloucester Breakwater Light or Dog Bar Breakwater Light was built to protect the important commerce of Gloucester Harbor from Nor'easters. Caring for this light could be dangerous when gale-swept waves broke over the breakwater and ice coated the granite blocks.

An estimated forty ships crashed into the breakwater at night during foul weather necessitating construction of the tripod beacon at the outward end of the breakwater.

Mother Ann's Cow

Mother Anne's Cow is a whistling buoy located near Mother Ann Rock. The rock, when viewed at the correct angle, appears to be the silhouette of a reclining Puritan woman. It is also believed locally that the formation represents the royal mother of King Charles I, Anne of Denmark, after whom Cape Ann is named.

When it was installed in 1905 Elizabeth Stuart Phelps (a prominent local writer and summer resident) complained that its shrilling noise kept her awake claiming she suffered from a "nervous ailment." In an attempt to be a good neighbor, the US Navy ordered the buoy silenced from May to October.

After Ms. Phelps' marriage to the Rev. Herbert Ward, the *Boston Record* reported, "Since her marriage, Mrs. Ward is much better, and the officer who had to remove the buoy has put it back with the assurance that next summer he will have no orders to disturb it."

Famous Resident

In 1880, American landscape painter Winslow Homer occupied the wooden two-story, Gothic Revival

Mother Ann

keeper's dwelling for a year as guest of keeper Charles Friend.

Theodore Parker Burbank

The picture below is of two lads sitting on what is thought to be "Mother Ann", a distinctive rock formation located along the shore near the lighthouse.

Painted by Winslow Homer in 1880

Station Stats
Station Established: 1832
Current Tower First Lit: 1890
Automated: 1986
Foundation Materials: Stone
Construction Materials: Brick
Tower Shape: Conical
Markings/Pattern: White with Black Lantern & Red roof
Original Lens: Fourth Order Fresnel, 1857

The Ghost Ship of Salem
Hark! an Evil Omen

The Reverend Cotton Mather was a prolific writer penning more than four hundred books and pamphlets. The recounting of the ghost ship tale comes from his "Maglia Christi Americana" and is set in the early 1670s. Poet John Greenleaf Whittier

used Mather's work as the basis for his poem about the "Ghost Ship of Salem."

Long they sat and talked together, - talked of wizards Satan-sold;
Of all ghostly sights and noises, - signs and wonders manifold;
Of the spectre-ship of Salem, with dead men in her shrouds,
Sailing sheer above the water. In the loom of morning cloud

Salem's main wharf was bustling with activity as passenger ship *Noah's Dove* was preparing to embark on its journey to England. Excitement along with apprehension filled the air as any sea voyage in the 1600s was a risky undertaking. In this era major concerns were: omens of a supernatural nature, strangers, harsh weather and travel at sea. It was against this backdrop that the ship's departure unfolded.

It is said a "strange" young couple arrived to make passage on the vessel Noah's Dove. The reason they were considered strange was not recorded however, that they made townsfolk leery was. Many took their presence as a "Bad Sign."

To intensify this atmosphere of doom a raven (considered an ill omen and   sign of impending death by people of the day) circled the crowd so to draw attention to itself and land on the minute hand of the town clock advancing it by ten minutes.

This combination of "Omens" puts the crowd on nervous edge. As the last passengers are boarding a fight breaks out among the assembled as family and friends attempt to prevent loved ones from boarding the ship.

Enter two strangers - husband and wife. She is obviously unhappy about being forced on board by her husband. This makes the crowd even uneasier.

Then, as if on signal, as soon as the strangers board the Noah's Dove a strong wing, then a gale picks up and the ship is briskly carried out to sea.

Soon the gale has turned into a fierce hurricane. The storm continues for three days. On the fourth day towns people awake to a beautiful sunny day. As they begin their daily routine a sail is spotted on the distant horizon.

The wind was brisk blowing from the land out to sea and the distant ship. An old sea captain is reported as say, "with the wind so strong from this quarter she will not reach town until the 'morrow."

The ship defied the wind by sailing directly into it and straight ahead towards the town. Folks on shore soon recognized it as the Noah's Dove and to their horror, recognized the now dead husband and his reluctant wife standing in an embrace on the ship's deck. The ship and her dead passengers and crew were sailing directly into the wind towards the town shore at an incredible speed.

Suddenly, with one huge thunderclap and lightning, the masts and ragged sails collapsed and the ship sank beneath the water; never to be seen again.

Boston Light (1716)

America's First Light Blown up by British –
Haunted by Many Ghosts

Boston Light located on seven acre Little Brewster Island in outer Boston Harbor. It was built in 1716 and was the first lighthouse to be built in the American colonies. In the same year, the town of Hull petitioned the General Assembly to appoint George Worthylake as the first light-keeper.

November 3, 1718 the first keeper of Boston Light, his wife, daughter and two men, drowned when their boat capsized as they were returning to the island from attending church in Boston.

The *Boston Newsletter* describes the accident:

"On Monday last the 3d currant an awful and lamentable Providence fell out here. Mr. George Worthylake, (Master of the Light-House upon Great

69

Brewster (called Beacon Island) at the entrance of the harbour of Boston), Anne his wife, Ruth their daughter, George Cutler, a servant, Shadwell their negro slave, and Mr. John Edge a passenger; being on the Lord's Day here at sermon, and going home in a sloop, dropt anchor near the landing place, and all got into a little boat or cannoo, designing to go on to shoar, but by accident overwhelmed it, so that they were drowned, and all found, and interred except George Cutler."

Ten days later, Captain Robert Saunders who was assigned *"to repair to Beacon Island & take care of the Light House till a keeper be chosen & appointed by the General Assembly."* and his assistant also drowned at Boston Light. The November 17, 1718 *Boston Newsletter* describes the second accident:

"There being a necessity to supply Mr. Worthylakes place to keep up the lights on that island, Capt. Robert Saunders and two others, viz [namely] John Chamberlin and one Brad[d]uck, were appointed to go down, who accordingly went on Fryday [November 14] last, to the Light House about three a clock, and a ship coming in from sea put out a waft [beckon]; and Capt. Saunders with the other two went on board her, and Capt. Saunders inquired, if they wanted a pilot, seeing they made a sign for them. The master said, no, he only wanted to know what news; whereupon Capt. Saunders told him, that if had known so much we would not have ventur'd aboard in such stormy weather, so returning to their boat to come on shore; a saw of wind overset her, Capt. Saunders & Bradduck both drowned, Mr. Chamberlin swam directly to the shore, but rested upon...rocks, ere he got on shore, where he laid before the fire and begun to revive, and is now lying sick in Boston."

Benjamin Franklin, then a 12-year old boy, was inspired to write a song about the drownings, naming it *The Light House Tragedy*. He printed handbills of the ballad and sold them in the streets of Boston.

In 1774 the British took over the island. They held it during the opening stage of the Revolutionary War and the Siege of Boston (April 19, 1775 until March 17, 1775) during which time the lighthouse was attacked and burnt on two occasions by Colonial forces.

March, 17 1776 the 11-month Siege of Boston ended when the Continental Army, under the command of George

Washington, fortified Dorchester Heights with cannon captured at Ticonderoga.

British General William Howe, who was commander of the British garrison and navy, was forced to decide between attack and retreat. To prevent what could have been a repeat of the Battle of Bunker Hill, Howe decided to retreat, withdrawing from Boston to Nova Scotia on March 17, 1776. Boston celebrates this date as Evacuation Day with parades and celebrations (coincidentally it is celebrated as St Patrick's Day also). Before sailing away, the British went ashore at Boston Light and blew up the lighthouse.

In 1783, the Massachusetts legislature provided $1,450 to rebuild the war-damaged tower with a seventy-five foot tall conical stone tower with walls 7 feet 6 inches thick at the base, tapering to 2 feet 6 inches at the top. The Light was completed in December of the same year

Until the late 1840's a cannon was used as the station's fog signal. **In 1850,** a fog bell, weighing nearly three-quarters of a ton, was installed. In 1872, a more modern fog trumpet was added, and fifteen years later a steam siren was put in place.

In 1851, the wooden interior tower stairs were removed and replaced with a metal stairway and the tower equipped with a new twenty-one-inch English parabolic reflectors. In 1859 the tower was raised fourteen feet to eighty-nine feet above ground in order to extend the light's range.

In 1856, the tower, which was developing cracks, was strengthened with a lining of brick and raised to its present height of 98 feet and a new lantern room was added along with a 12-sided second order Fresnel lens of 1,800,000 candlepower. Its flashing white light is visible for more than twenty-seven miles out to sea. The light has burned brightly continuously ever since, except for blackouts during World War 2.

The U.S. Coast Guard operates this light station with America's last resident lighthouse keepers attending the lens.

Notwithstanding the warning supplied by the light and fog signal during rough weather, several ships have come to their end at the doorstep of the Boston light:

- The *Miranda*, 1861a square-rigger, ran on the rocks in a snowstorm and left but twelve survivors.
- The *Fanny Pike* went ashore on Shag Rocks in 1882, Keeper Thomas Bates rowed out and took the crew safely off the ledge.
- The schooner *Calvin F. Baker* in 1898 also smashed onto rocks near the lighthouse; three crewmen froze to death in the rigging.
- When the USS *Alacrity* was wrecked off the island on February 3, 1918, Keeper Jennings and his assistants rescued all 24 men.

The Ghost Walk - Haunted Waterway
Scores of other ships have wrecked on and near Little Brewster Island over the centuries and New England mariners tell of an area they call the "Ghost Walk." The Ghost Walk is an area several miles east of Little Brewster Island. It is claimed that one cannot hear Boston Light's signal in the Ghost Walk. New England folklore considers the area to be haunted by the souls of

lost sailors who perished attempting to escape storms by entering Boston Harbor.

In 1893 the Massachusetts Institute of Technology sent students to live on the island, to experiment with various types of foghorns in an attempt to find one that would penetrate the "Ghost Walk" several miles to the east. They were unable determine or explain why this phenomenon was happening. The mystery as to why continues to be unsolved to this day.

Classical Music Loving Ghost

This ghost of this ancient sailor has been seen from time to time and his presence is signaled by an unexplained cold draft, even on hot summer nights. The lighthouse cat hissing at an empty chair rocking on its own is another hint of the ghost's presence. This apparition has a particular dislike for rock and other loud "modern" music. Guardsmen reported the radio would "Jump to the bandwidth of a classical music station" on its own accord.

More Reports of Ghosts and Curses

There are other mysteries associated with Boston Light. John Ford, a local lighthouse enthusiast, makes frequent trips to Boston Light and has stayed overnight in the keeper's house on several occasions.

"I can't say who or what it is, but there is a ghost or something out there," Ford asserts. *"But,"* he adds, *"It's not a scary kind of ghost."*

Double Tragedy Ghosts?

Could the spirit(s) stalking Little Brewster be Captain Worthylake, the first keeper of Boston Light or perhaps Robert Saunders the second keeper who after only a few days on the job were drowned?

"It could be any one of the old keepers," Ford says. *"The men—and women—who kept the lighthouses were very dedicated and very possessive of their lights. There are all kinds of stories about haunted lighthouses. I think it's just some of the old keepers--still on the job."*

Theodore Parker Burbank

Station Stats
Station Established: 1716 First Lit: 1783
Automated: YES 1998
Foundation Materials: Granite Ledge
Construction Materials: Stone/Brick lining Tower Shape: Conical
Markings/Pattern: White with 5 steel bands and Black trim
Original Lens: Tallow candles 1716

Visitor Information
Little Brewster Island is part of Boston Harbor Islands State Park.
For info (781) 740-4290. For harbor cruises lists and schedules call
the Greater Boston Area Visitors Center at (781) 536-4100.

The Boston Light tower is open for group tours during spring,
summer, and fall by arrangement only: call 617-223-8666. Little
Brewster Island is open to private boaters on Fridays, Saturdays, and
Sundays from 12:30 PM to 3:00 PM for drop-off and pick-up only.
No docking. Boaters must anchor off shore.

Nixes Mate Island,

The Disappearing Island

Nixes Mate, also known as Nixes Island, Nix's Mate and Nick's Mate, is a very small island in the Boston Harbor Islands National Recreation Area. The "island" is situated about 6 miles offshore of downtown Boston in Nubble Channel a/k/a the Narrows, and the entrance to Boston Harbor. The island is only 200 square feet in size and rises to a height of 10 feet above sea level at high tide.

A prominent black and white wooden pyramid beacon, resting atop a granite base, increases the island's height to 20 feet. The base was erected by Boston Marine Society in 1805 and is managed by the United States Coast Guard.

Pirates Executed on the Island

It was the custom in the 1700s to hang pirates and other maritime criminals on this island located on the starboard side of the main channel into Boston Harbor. They were to hang there to illustrate and to serve as an example to all approaching Boston from away of the severe punishment metered out to wrong doers.

Can you imagine the reaction of weary immigrants as they arrived in Boston Harbor being greeted by corpses blowing in the wind! Certainly not the welcoming message the Statue of Liberty would portray two hundred fifty miles south and one hundred years later.

In 1726, upon the arrest of William Fly, the infamous pirate, who headed the crew of the *Elizabeth* in a mutiny while on a voyage from Jamaica to Guinea, and threw overboard the mate and captain. Officials brought him to Boston where he was executed. His body was then gibbeted (Hanged in an iron cage) on Nixe's Mate to serve as a warning to sailors not to turn to piracy. Before Fly's execution, he famously scolded the hangman for incorrectly securing his noose. His body as well as those of two other pirates were buried on the island.

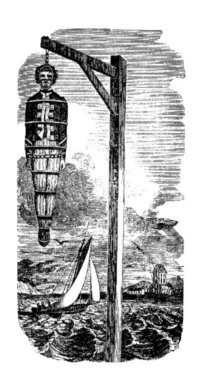

Wait a minute, how could you possibly bury three persons on an island the equivalent in size to a 10' X 20' shed and still have room to perform executions? A clue to the answer to that question lies in the island's name. It is said that before it was called Nix's Mate the island bore the name of its owner a Mr. Gallop who used the then sizable island for the grazing of his sheep.

The Curse of Nixe's Mate

The demise of the once sizeable island is said to have been caused by the curse of a seaman who was executed there; the mate of a Captain Nixe. History has not recorded the name of the hapless Captain Nixe's mate. What is known is that he was accused of a capital crime, killing his captain while at sea, of which he vehemently professed his innocence. "God, show that I am innocent. Let this island sink and prove to these people that I have never stained my hands with human blood." All ignored his protestations and he was taken out to the then 12 acre island that would later reference his life and hung by his neck until he was dead.

Before the hangman sprung the trap door that would send Nixe's mate into eternity and posterity he screamed a curse into the salty wind: "I curse this island and those who condemn me and this island will disappear beneath the sea in proof of my innocence."

Remarkably, soon after, the island began to diminish in size and before long it would be completely under water at high tide. Was this proof of Nixe's mate's innocence, or was the disappearance of the island just a coincidence?

By 1832 the island had shrunk in size to a point where it presented a severe hazard to navigation causing the US government to purchase what was left of the island and construct the granite base and build a wooden pyramid on top to support a beacon.

A few years after the beacon was built it was struck by lightning and demolished. Was this a part of the sailor's curse?

Other Versions

Some questions this legend as the island apparently bore the name Nixes Island as early as the1630s, long before anyone was executed in Massachusetts for murder or piracy.

Another form of the legend states that Nix was a pirate, who in 1680, sailed into Boston to bury several bags of coin on the island. Nix then murdered his companions, and buried them along with the treasure; dead men tell no tales.

The commuter ferry from Boston to Hingham and Quincy passes by the island daily and provides a good platform from which to view the tiny island and its beacon.

Long Island Head Light – Fort Strong

Woman in Scarlet

WWII-era postcard showing Long Island Light, the Keeper's House and Fort Strong

The light was established in 1819, one hundred and three years after Boston Light, as Boston's second lighthouse. The twenty-foot stone tower was known as "Inner Harbor Light". It was the second of the four Boston lights. In 1900 the fourth and current lighthouse was built further away from the expanding Fort Strong to minimize the affect of the concussions from its cannons.

The Ghost of the Women in Scarlet

The island is also the residence of one of the harbor's most famous ghosts, the Woman in Scarlet. Edward Rowe Snow, author and chronicler of New England's coast, wrote of this phantom in his 1935 book, "The Islands of Boston Harbor."

At the close of the American Revolution, the British still had several ships languishing in Boston Harbor. In an effort to encourage their departure, the Colonial Army began to bombard the British vessels from Fort Strong and other placements in Boston Harbor.

Aboard one of the departing British ships were the newly weds Mary and William Burton. During the bombardment Mary was hit in the head by a cannon ball and mortally wounded. Miraculously, the cannon ball did not kill her instantly, as one would expect, and she lingered on for several days. Fighting through excruciating pain and bouts of unconsciousness, she pleaded with her husband to not bury her at sea. Her dying wish was to be buried on shore.

William was faced with a dilemma; how, in the face of the hostilities, could he get his wife ashore in the face of the cannon fire. Somehow, William received permission to go ashore at Long Island, with his wife wrapped in a red blanket ,where he buried her in a grave somewhere between the Fort and the Lighthouse.

William made a rude headstone out of a piece of driftwood and swore that he would return to Boston and give her a proper marker. He never returned.

But Mary apparently refuses to be forgotten. Visitors to the island often report seeing a woman with "muddy-gray skin" and wearing a scarlet cloak stumbling about on Long Island Point. Blood is seen streaming down her red cloak from a gaping hole in the back of her head - the exact spot where the cannon fire had smashed her skull.
Snow recounted two occasions when the ghost of Mary Burton appeared. The first was reported by a group of shipwrecked fishermen in 1804. They heard a moan or wail followed by the apparition of a woman in a red cloak coming toward them. Blood streamed from a wound in her head as she disappeared over a hill.

In 1891 the ghost made another appearance to a soldier at Fort Strong, which neighbored the lighthouse station. The soldier described a similarly moaning woman in red.

Keeper's Last Toboggan Ride

There's also a macabre story connected with the last keeper of Long Island Head Lighthouse, Edwin Tarr. In January of 1918 Tarr died while sitting in a chair looking out over the water. A soldier, who served as a pallbearer, later told an unusual story to Edward Rowe Snow.

Keeper Tarr's funeral was held in the keeper's house at the top of the hill next to the lighthouse. During the funeral an ice storm struck and left the hill coated with ice. The four pallbearers attempted to negotiate the slippery slope, but they soon lost control of the coffin, which went skidding down the path. As the coffin started to gain speed, the four men jumped on board and rode it like a toboggan until it came to rest at the head of the island's wharf.

No one has reported experiencing this but might it be possible that on cold snowy and slippery days the spirit of keeper Tarr might return to experience the fun of his "last ride."

History

The light was established in 1819, one hundred and three years after Boston Light, as Boston's second lighthouse. The twenty-foot stone tower was known as "Inner Harbor Light". It was the second of the four Boston lights. In 1900 the fourth and current lighthouse was built further away from the expanding Fort Strong to minimize the affect of the concussions from its cannons.

The current brick tower is the fourth lighthouse on the island. The light was first established largely as a result of a study conducted by the Boston Marine Society, which had built the daybeacon on Nixes Mate 14 years earlier. It was a 20-foot (6.1 m) stone tower known as "Inner Harbor Light".

It was the second of the four Boston lights—103 years after Boston Light, but ten years before the first daybeacon at the site of Deer IslandLight, and before The Graves Light, built in 1905.

The stone tower fell into disrepair and was replaced by one of the earliest cast iron lighthouse structures, thirty-four feet tall (pictured below). In 1857, a fourth order Fresnel lens replaced the lamps and reflectors, which had been in place. During the next twenty years it sustained damage in a number of storms. In 1881, it was replaced again, by a conical cast iron structure and a new wood keeper's house. Fort Strong was significantly enlarged around the start of the 20th century and it was necessary to move the lighthouse to a location out of the way of the concussion from the guns, so the current brick tower was constructed in 1900-01. Remnants of the fort can be seen to the southeast of the light in the satellite views available by clicking on the coordinates.

The Coast Guard discontinued the light in 1982, but reconsidered the decision in 1985, and installed a modern, solar powered system. It received a major refurbishing in the summer of 1998.[1]

Long Island Head Light was added to the National Register of Historic Places as Long Island Head Light on June 15, 1987.

Station Stats
Station established: 1819
Current lighthouse tower built: 1901
Deactivated: 1982-85
Relighted 1985
Construction material: Brick
Tower height: 52 feet
Height of focal plane: 120 feet
Earlier optic: Fourth-order Fresnel lens (1857)
Present optic: VLB-44 (LED), solar powered (below)
Characteristic: Flashing white every 2.5 seconds

USS Constitution

Most Haunted Ship in the World?

Oil painting by Gordon Grant circa 1917

The USS Constitution has the reputation as being the most haunted ships in the world. Sailors on naval vessels moored nearby, in past years, reported sightings of spirit forms of men in outdated Navy uniform walking her decks.

That should not be surprising because the Constitution has had a long and bloody history. Many good men have perished on her decks, both in battle and while on duty at sea. Operating a full-rigged military sailing ship is dangerous duty, even in the modern navy.

Ghost of First Seaman to Die Aboard the *Constitution*
Among the first crewmembers to die on the *Constitution's* decks was Seaman Neil Harvey. The man fell asleep while on watch and failed to alert his ship to the approaching French Frigate *L'Insurgent* while in the West Indies in 1799.

The French vessel attacked catching the Constitution by surprise. Commodore Thomas Truxton, the first man to command the *Constitution*, ordered an officer to run a sword through Harvey's gut.

After the battle, Truxton had Harvey's body tied over the end of a cannon and blown to pieces as a warning to the other sailors. They say Harvey's spirit has haunted the ship ever since.

The *Constellation*, then rigged as a 36-gun frigate, engaged the French ship *Vengeance*, 52 guns, off Guadeloupe Island on Feb. 2, 1800. The *Constellation* won the five-hour nighttime  battle, with a loss of 14 lives and adding additional spirits to haunt the ship.

Two sailors while aboard murdered an unidentified young surgeon's assistant in 1822. It is said that this boy's spirit joined the others that haunt the *Constitution*.

With the rumors of increased spirit sightings began circulating in 1955, Lt. Commander Allen R. Brougham went aboard the ship with a photographer to see for himself. The two set up on a spot overlooking the ship's wheel. At about midnight, the figure of a nineteenth century navy captain appeared long enough to be captured on film. The picture shows a man in gold epaulets reaching for his sword. He is believed to be the ghost of Captain Truxton.

Other sightings include the figure of a sailor running across the gun deck. Another seaman has been seen wandering around the gun deck. Others say they have heard the sounds of cries and moans in the hold, the sounds of unseen people running, and even smelled gun smoke.

Then there is the ghost of Carl Hansen, a night watchman who worked on the *Constitution* until he was replaced by an alarm system in 1963. His spirit has been observed playing cards on the lower decks. A priest claimed to have once been given a tour of the ship by a man who was not part of the staff. As the story is told, the guide fit the description of Hanson.

Over the years, the *Constitution* has gone through so many restorations that few, if any of the original wooden parts of the ship remain. But the ghosts of men who died on her decks have obviously chosen to remain.

"We took ghosts so seriously on Constitution," said Petty Officer 1st Class Pete Robertson, who served aboard the ship from 2001 to 2004. *"Unless you were a brand new crewmember, you didn't mess around with that stuff. You didn't make jokes about it ... You didn't even try to scare each other because people were terrified – a lot of people were terrified to stand watch on the ship."*

Robertson remembers watching objects rolling on the deck for no apparent reason. One night, a 24-pound cannonball rolled to the left, the right, and then back from whence it came, even though the ship was completely still.

"There was no way the ship moves that way," he said. *"It was moving in ways a cannonball just shouldn't move."*

Former Seaman Allie Thorpe, who was aboard the ship between 2002 and 2005, never saw a ghost but she definitely felt a presence.

"It would feel like there was somebody there with you," she said. *"It would feel like somebody was walking up behind you and blowing on your neck."*

It's not only the ship where spirits allegedly dwell. About 100 yards away from the *Constitution*, there is an old brick barracks in the Navy yard. Each room has a rocking chair.

"The rocking chair, if you moved it to the middle of the room and left it there and just watched it, it would go from sitting completely still to a full on rock on its own," she said.

Theodore Parker Burbank

Skeleton Mooncurser
Attracts Ghost Ship

USS Salem - 139

Most Haunted Modern Ship?

Haunted by many spirits

The *USS Salem CA-139* was unofficially nicknamed "The Sea Witch" and its official nickname was "Pride of the Sixth Fleet." In 1953 the nickname changed to *"The Haunted Ship"* following the period it served as a hospital ship after one of the world's most powerful earthquakes, the "Ionian Earthquake", destroyed the Greek islands of the Ionian Sea. The ship has been reputed to be haunted ever since.

From August 9th through the 12th four major earthquakes and 113 aftershocks left the islands a dramatic scene of devastation and tragedy. Eighty percent of its population reportedly died in the holocaust.

Served as a Morgue for Victims

Ships from nations of the world converged upon the scene to render whatever aid was possible. The Salem's freezers in the ship's 3rd Mess Hall were used as makeshift morgue for an estimated 400 victims of the quake. Visitors and sailors have reported hearing what sounds as though medical gurneys are being wheeled about the mess hall. Many others have reported hearing voices and some say they experienced a definite sense of being pushed into the freezers.

Where Onboard Sighting Have Occurred

2nd Mess Hall - This area was used as the burn victim's quarters. An apparition of a face with burns has been witnessed here. A Shadow Person has been seen here and in the Ward Room.

The voice of a woman yelling; "Get Out. Get out, Ouch!" is thought to be the spirit of a female "Ionian Earthquake" survivor in labor. Twenty-one babies were delivered aboard the Salem while in the Ionian Sea. Many have heard a barking dog here.

Captain and Admirals Quarters – A ghostly presence walking up the stairs between 3pm – 6pm. Also the feeling of pressure while sitting in the chairs.

The Ward Room – People being touched while others claims to hear a loud "um hum um hum."

Naval Dentist Office – Dental drills are heard and none are present.

The Hallways – Footsteps have been heard throughout the ship, a dog barking (but never found) has been heard. People walking around in navy blue, possibly denim, clothing started to be reported once the #2 Gun Turrets were restored. The voice of a little girl giggling and laughing.

Flag Bridge – Naval officer seen. Figure in white seen from parking lot of ship.

Galley – Sound of clanking dishes and pots and pans being jostled about.

Bakery – Banging sounds and vibrations

Head – One way swinging stall doors unlock by themselves and open the wrong way

Anchor Room - A headless man makes a silent appearance. He is said to have met his demise when the ship's anchor was lowered; inadvertently decapitating him.

Berthing Area – Ghostly figures silently appear and then disappear.

Engine Room – The ghost of a restoration volunteer who suffered a stroke and died on board appears going about his work.

Ghostly Tour Guide

An elderly volunteer was found dead in the Anchor room while the ship was berthed in Quincy. He was said to be always pleasant, happy and eager to help. His ghost began appearing a few years ago. He would-appear, answer tourists' questions and retell various stories of the Salem's history as he showed off the ship. Different visitors to the Salem have said he is kind and helpful, but will suddenly vanish as they turn to leave the ship.

The Salem is now berthed at the Boston Harbor Shipyard and Marina in East Boston,

History

USS Salem was laid down on 4 July 1945 by the Bethlehem Steel Co.'s Fore River Shipyard, Quincy, Mass.; launched on 25 March 1947; and commissioned on 14 May 1949. Her main batteries held the world's first automatic 8" guns and were the first 8" naval guns to use cased ammunition instead of shell and bag loading.

Stats:

Keel laid: July 4, 1945 - Launched: March 25, 1947

Commissioned: May 14, 1949

Decommissioned: January 30, 1959

Builder: Bethlehem Steel, Quincy, Mass.

Propulsion system: geared turbines; 120,000 shaft horsepower

Propellers: four - Length: 716.5 feet

Beam: 75.5 feet - Draft: 26 feet

Displacement: approx. 20,450 tons full load

Speed: 33 knots

Armament: nine 8-inch 55 caliber guns from three triple mounts, twelve 5-inch 38 caliber guns from six twin mounts, 24 3-inch 50 caliber guns

Crew: 60 officers and 1,240 enlisted

Ghost Ship Still Sails the Seas

Castle Island - Fort Independence
"Southie's Sea Serpent" and
"The Cask of Amontillado"

Sea Serpent Spotted off Castle Island

"August 15, 1818, two sentries report sighting a sea serpent swim past Castle Island. Their superior, Colonel Harris, verifies the sighting, as does a resident, James Prince, who later describes the creature thus: 'His head appeared about three feet out of the water; I counted thirteen bunches on his back---my family thought there were fifteen—he passed three times at a moderate rate across the bay.... I had seven distinct views of him from the long beach so call and at some of them the animal was not more than a hundred yards distance.'"

"The Cask of Amontillado"

A persistent, though mostly apocryphal, story involving Fort Independence was allegedly the inspiration behind one of Edgar Allan Poe's most well known works.

A monument outside the west battery of the fort marks the grave of Lieutenant Robert F. Massie, who was killed in a duel there on December 25, 1817. According to folklorist Edward Rowe Snow,

Massie was so popular with the soldiers stationed at Fort Independence that they took out their frustration on his killer, Lieutenant Gustavus Drane, by walling him up within a vault in the fort.

Edgar Allan Poe, while serving with the 1st United States Artillery Regiment at Fort Independence purportedly heard the tale and was inspired, according to Snow, to write *The Cask of Amontillado*.

The legend that purportedly inspired Poe is not entirely accurate. The duel did in fact take place, but the victor, Lieutenant Drane, was not murdered by the fort's soldiers but continued in his military career and was later promoted to the rank of captain. After the Second World War, Lieutenant Massie's remains were moved to the cemetery at Fort Devens in Ayer, Massachusetts.

History

Fort Independence is a granite star fort that provided harbor defenses for Boston, Massachusetts. Located on Castle Island, Fort Independence is the oldest continuously fortified site of English origin in the United States. The first primitive wooden fortification was placed on the site in 1634 and replaced in 1701 with a fort made of brick. Castle William was named in honor of King William III of England

In the years leading up to the American Revolution, Castle William became a refuge for British officials during periods of unrest and rioting in Boston. Violence in the wake of events such as the Stamp Act crisis in 1765 and the Boston Massacre in 1770 forced provincial leaders and British soldiers to take shelter within the fort.

It was re-built when the British abandoned it during the American Revolution; Castle William was renamed Fort Adams

and later Fort Independence. The existing granite fort was constructed between 1833 and 1851. Today it is preserved as a state park and fires occasional ceremonial salutes.

Fort Warren on George's Island

The Lady in Black

The construction of the fort began in 1833 as a key component in the Harbor's defense system and was completed in 1857.

The fort is located on twenty-eight acre Georges Island and is ideally situated to protect the main shipping channels and entrance into Boston. The fort was named for Dr. Joseph Warren, the patriot leader who sent Paul Revere and William Dawes to alert Lexington and Concord on the night before the battles there that began the American Revolution. Dr. Warren was killed at the Battle of Bunker Hill.

The Ghost of the "Lady in Black"

During the American Civil War, a Confederate Army Lieutenant named Andrew Lanier was captured at Roanoke Island and sent to Fort Warren with several thousand other captured Confederate soldiers. Somehow, he got word of his imprisonment to his new wife. Being a determined woman, she headed to Boston confident she would be able to find a way to free her love.

Clever Plan Conceived

Upon arrival in Boston she concocted a plan. She would cut her hair and disguised herself as a man and, by some means, managed to find her way onto George's Island, into the fort and to her husband's prison cell.

The plan worked quite well and apparently the pistol she was carrying convinced the guards of the wisdom in their releasing him to his wife.

Her clever plan seemed to be working just fine as they scurried through the fort's dark dungeons and the small boat she had hidden on the shore in which to complete their escape.

Colonel Dimick, commander of the fort, was notified of the impending escape; he sounded a general alarm, and the newly weds were now about to be captured

Plan Backfires

However the bold Mrs. Lanier was not to go easily, she was determined not to be caught; especially after all she had endured and so close to freedom. The Union Army pursuers were closing in fast and they best hurry as the couple was very close to their little boat. They were almost there. Mrs. Lanier stopped, turned and fired her old pistol at her Union pursuers. It exploded in her hand; the shards instantly killed her husband as he stood next to her.

Her husband dead, and now captured, Mrs. Lanier imprisoned and sentenced to hang for treason. She requested that she not be hanged dressed as a man but rather as a woman. There were no other women at the fort from whom a dress could be obtained; so some black robes were fashioned for her to wear on the gallows.

Another Version of the Legend

According to Edward Rowe Snow, famous historian, the events unfolded thusly:

"Mrs. Lanier received a letter from her husband that he had been imprisoned at Fort Warren. She was compelled to free him, making an epic journey from Georgia to Hull, Massachusetts and the home of a Confederate sympathizer. Hull is only about a mile away from George's Island. Mrs. Lanier systematically observed the fort with a spyglass, and on a stormy night in January 1862, had rowed across to George's Island and went ashore.

She cut her hair short and dressed as a man, and brought with her an old pistol and small pickaxe. She made her way to the dungeon cells, and from outside the fort signaled to her husband by whistling an obscure southern tune, to which he signaled back.

Mrs. Lanier was able to squeeze through the slit-window of his cell, and was then hidden by the Confederate soldiers. With the use of the pickaxe, the soldiers contrived to tunnel to the center of the fort, and then overtake the guards and obtain weapons.

The tunnel took several weeks to dig, and on the eve of finishing the tunnel, a sharp blow of the pick had alerted a guard. The alarm was sounded, and the tunnel quickly discovered. As each of the Confederate soldiers was removed from the tunnel, a tally was taken. When all the prisoners were accounted for, Mrs. Lanier was to spring from the tunnel and capture a Union officer with the old pistol. Mrs. Lanier succeeded in surprising the officer, but he slapped the pistol from her hand.

The pistol went off and the bullet struck and killed her husband. As punishment for her deeds, Mrs. Lanier was condemned to death by hanging. Her final request was to be given female clothing, and a search of the fort produced nothing but some old black robes. She was executed in these robes and buried on George's Island."

The "Lady in Black" still haunts the fort.

Accounts vary, but usually include a ghostly female apparition in long black robes. There is even a court martial case on record of a man who was on guard duty at Castle Island long ago and deserted his post because he "was being chased by a lady in long dark dress."

In another creepy occurrence, three soldiers were said to have been walking near the entrance of the fort and there before them were the impressions of five woman's footprints – leading from nowhere and starting nowhere – in the freshly-fallen, undisturbed snow.

Ten years before World War II, a certain sergeant from Fort Banks was climbing to the top of the ladder which leads to the Corridor of Dungeons when he heard a voice warning him, saying: "Don't come in here!" Needless to say, he did not venture further. There actually are on record court-martial cases of men who have shot at ghost-like figures while on sentry duty, and one poor man deserted his post, claiming he had been chased by the lady of the black robes.

Then there's the one about the poker game that was held for years in the fort's ordnance room. One night at 10:00, while all men that were on the island were in the room playing in the game, a large stone was rolled the entire length of the storeroom. The next time the men played the game, the same thing happened! The tradition of the poker game was soon abandoned and the Lady in Black was blamed!

To this day, reported sightings are not uncommon and several online forums include descriptions of people's personal encounters with this shadowy specter. But is it really the Lady in Black or just a figment of an over-stimulated imagination? Perhaps we will never know...

The origin of the John Brown song
By Edward Rowe Snow

With the Civil War came many patriotic songs and hymns. Fort Warren was the birthplace of the greatest of them all. The famous Yankee song "John Brown's Body," was the product of the 2nd Infantry or Tiger Battalion and came into being while the men were quartered at Georges Island. The Tiger Battalion arrived at Fort Warren on April 29, 1861.

When they landed on the island, the members found great heaps of earth lying around inside the parade ground, and it was made clear to the men that their first job would be to put the fortress into proper shape for military occupancy.

Singing seemed to be the best way for the men to pass their time while working on the pick and shovel, and all the popular songs of the day echoed across the parade ground.

After the work was completed, the men gathered in the casemates and sang far into the night. Religious hymns were popular, and the favorite hymn sung at the fort grew to be "Say Brothers, Will You Meet Us?" From this hymn sung time and time again, came the tune which eventually became "John Brown's Body."

The man who lead the raid on Harper's Ferry had a Scotch namesake in the Tiger Battalion. John Brown always joined in the fun at the fort, and when it was realized that he had the same name as the abolitionist hanged near Harper's Ferry, the others lost no time in making him the object of their fun.

While the song "John Brown's Body" was still in its infancy, the 12th Massachusetts Regiment, commanded by Fletcher Webster, came to Fort Warren. In a short time the tune was known by the whole company.

One Sunday night the regiment band at a joint dress parade electrified the gathering by striking up "John Brown's Body." This was the first time the song was ever played by a military band.

The 14th Regiment came to the fort, and they also enjoyed singing the song even after the Tigers had left the island. When the 14th went to Washington, Abraham Lincoln and Julia Ward Howe visited the camp of the Massachusetts soldiers. The stirring strains of "John Brown's Body" so moved Lincoln that he asked Julia Ward Howe to compose a hymn from the tune. "The Battle Hymn of the Republic" was her inspired answer.

The crowds went wild everywhere when they heard the magical strains of "John Brown's Body," and the melody soon reached the far corners of the Union. The great value and inspiration it was to the Northern troops will probably never be fully realized.

Edward Rowe Snow (1902-1982)

A granite memorial dedicated to famed historian, author and "Flying Santa to lighthouse keepers," Edward Rowe Snow is located at Fort Warren where he conducted tours for many years. He was the president of the Society for the Preservation of Fort Warren and led the fight to save the fort for future generations.

Theodore Parker Burbank

Ghostly Lovers

Minot's Ledge Light

Historically Haunted "Lover's Light"

The Replacement Light Operational

The Original Lighthouse Circa 1850

Demon on the Ledge

Well before the arrival of European settlers the native Quonahassitis Indians believed that a demonic spirit or ghost they called Hobomock dwelt among the submerged jagged rocks and, if provoked would unleash violent storms. They would paddle to the ledge when the seas were calm and at low tide when the rocks were closest to the surface to make offerings to the "Wicked One."

The ledge we now call Minots Ledge, a/k/a Cohasset Rocks, is named after George Minot, a prominent Boston businessman, who lost a valuable ship and all of its cargo on the ledge in 1754. The Ledge is barely visible below the sea and lies a mile from shore, three miles south of the entrance to Boston Harbor. It has been the nemesis of mariners for centuries.

The first recorded wreck here occurred in 1695 and up to 1750 eighty ships and more than 400 lives had been lost on the treacherous rocks. In 1843 a report detailing the need for a lighthouse on the Ledge listed forty recent major wrecks and

99

stating that the ledge was "annually the scene of the most heart-rending disasters."

Haunted by Many Spirits

The evil spirit of "Hobomock" was the first reported supernatural being residing on the Ledge but certainly was not the last. Lobstermen report hearing cries for help and moaning coming from the area near the Light. Could this be the spirits of some of the several hundred souls who lost their lives in shipwrecks on the Ledge? Might the cries include the souls lost in the tragic wreck of the *St John* of Galway in 1849?

More than one keeper reported the presence of two phantom figures in the lantern room, and unexplained taps on their shoulders, knocks and the ringing of a phantom bell were often heard in the middle of the night. Many lighthouse personnel swore that on calm, sunny days, if one looked at the reflection of the tower in the water, the images of the two drowned assistant keepers would appear in the doorway

Subsequent Keepers at the Light reported being convinced it was the ghosts of the assistant keepers who were the ones aaSQcontinually cleaning and polishing the glass lenses.

A monument to the victims of the *St John* wreck overlooks the harbor from Cohasset's Central Cemetery.

The crew of Portuguese fishermen reported seeing a figure hanging from the lighthouse's ladder shouting at them in Portuguese "Stay away, stay away"; the drowned Assistant Keeper Joseph Antoine was a native of Portugal.

Tragedy at Cohasset
Do their Spirits Linger Still on Minot's Ledge?

The immigrant ship St. John sailing from Galway to Boston at the height of the Great Irish Famine, was wrecked at the entrance to Cohasset Harbor on October 7, 1849. Ninety-nine souls died in the incident.

We have assembled several contemporaneous accounts of the wreck.

Henry David Thoreau's account of the St John wreck

We left Concord, Massachusetts on Tuesday, October 9th, 1849. On reaching Boston, we found that the Provincetown steamer, which should have got in the day before, had not yet arrived, on account of a violent storm; and, as we noticed in the streets a handbill headed, "Death! 145 lives lost at Cohasset!" we decided to go by way of Cohasset.

We found many Irish in the cars, going to identify bodies and to sympathize with the survivors, and also to attend the funeral which was to take place in the afternoon;--and when we arrived at Cohasset, it appeared that nearly all the passengers were bound for the beach, which was about a mile distant, and many other persons were flocking in from the neighboring country. There were several hundreds of them streaming off over Cohasset common in that direction--some on foot and some in wagons--and, among them, were some sportsmen in their hunting jackets, with their guns and game-bags and dogs.

As we passed the grave-yard we saw a large hole, like a cellar, freshly dug there, and, just before reaching the shore, by a pleasantly winding and rocky road, we met several hay-riggings and farm wagons coming away toward the meeting-house, each loaded with three large, rough deal boxes. We did not need to ask what was in them. The owners of the wagons were made the undertakers. Many horses in carriages were fastened to the fences near the shore, and, for a mile or more, up and down, the beach was covered with people looking out for bodies and examining the fragments of the wreck.

There was a small island called Brush Island, with a hut on it, lying just off the shore. This is said to be the rockiest shore in Massachusetts, from Nantasket to Scituate--hard sienitic rocks, which the waves have laid bare, but have not been able to crumble. It has been the scene of many a shipwreck.

On the whole, it was not so impressive a scene as I might have expected. If I had found one body cast upon the beach in some lonely place, it would have affected me more. I sympathized rather with the winds and waves, as if to toss and mangle these poor human bodies was the order of  the day. If this was the law of Nature, why waste any time in awe or pity? If the last day were come, we should not think so much about the separation of friends or the blighted prospects of individuals. I saw that corpses might be multiplied, as on the field of battle, till they no longer affected us in any degree, as exceptions to the common lot of humanity. Take all the graveyards together, they are always the majority.

It is the individual and private that demands our sympathy. A man can attend but one funeral in the course of his life, can behold but one corpse. Yet I saw that the inhabitants of the shore would be not a little affected by this event.

They would watch there many days and nights for the sea to give up its dead, and their imaginations and sympathies would supply the place of mourners far away, who, as yet, knew not of the wreck.

Many days after this, something white was seen floating on the water by one who was sauntering on the beach. It was approached in a boat, and found to be the body of a woman, which had risen in an upright position, whose white cap was blown back with the wind. I saw that the beauty of the shore itself was wrecked for many a lonely walker there, until he could perceive, at last, how its beauty was enhanced by wrecks like this, and it acquired thus a rarer and sublime beauty still.

Why care for these dead bodies? They really have no friends but the worms or fishes. Their owners were coming to the New World, as Columbus and the Pilgrims did, they were within a mile of its shores; but, before they could reach it, they emigrated to a newer world than ever Columbus dreamed of, yet one of whose existence we believe that there is far more universal and convincing evidence--though it has not yet been discovered by science--than Columbus had of this; not merely mariners' tales and some paltry drift-wood and sea-weed, but a continual drift and instinct to all our shores. I saw their empty hulks that came to land; but they themselves, meanwhile, were cast upon some shore yet further west, toward which we are all tending, and which we shall reach at last, it may be through storm and darkness, as they did.

No doubt, we have reason to thank God, that they have not been "shipwrecked into life again." The mariner who makes the safest port in Heaven, perchance, seems to his friends on earth to be shipwrecked, for they deem Boston harbor the better place; though, perhaps, invisible to them, a skillful pilot comes to meet him, and the fairest and balmiest gales blow off that coast, his good ship makes the halcyon days, and he kisses the shore in rapture there, while his old hulk tosses in the surf here.

It is hard to part with one's body, but no doubt, it is easy enough to do without it when once it is gone. All their plans and hopes burst like a bubble! Infants by the score dashed on the rocks by the

103

enraged Atlantic Ocean! No, no! If the St. John did not make her port, she has been telegraphed there. The strongest wind cannot stagger a Spirit; it is a Spirit's breath. A just man's purpose cannot be split on any Grampus or material rock, but itself will split rocks till it succeeds.

I saw in Cohasset, separated from the sea only by a narrow beach, a handsome but shallow lake of some four hundred acres, which, I was told, the sea had tossed over the beach in a great storm in the spring, and, after the alewives had passed into it, it had stopped up its outlet, and now the alewives were dying by thousands, and the inhabitants were apprehending a pestilence as the water evaporated. It had five rocky islets in it.

This rocky shore is called Pleasant Cove, on some maps; on the map of Cohasset, that name appears to be confined to the particular cove where I saw the wreck of the St. John. The ocean did not look, now, as if any were ever shipwrecked in it; it was not grand and sublime, but beautiful as a lake. Not a vestige of a wreck was visible, nor could I believe that the bones of many a shipwrecked man were buried in that pure sand.

From The Galway (Ireland) Vindicator

Awful Shipwreck at Minot's Ledge -
Loss of *St. John* of Galway

About One Hundred Drowned - Men, Women and Children

We are indebted to our much respected friends from the Messrs Train & Co., the extensive Shipping and Emigration Agents of Liverpool, for the following melancholy intelligence, as also to our valued friend, John Moore, Esq., Post Office Pack-inspector of Boston, and formerly a citizen of Galway: -

The brig St. John, Capt. Oliver, from Galway, the property of Mr. H. Comerford, of this town [Galway], anchored inside of Minot's Ledge, Saturday, Sept. 5th. At about 7 o'clock a.m., on Sunday morning, she dragged her anchors and struck the rocks.

The following particulars of her loss, together with that of 99 of her passengers and crew, is gleaned from the various persons who witnessed the disaster: -

The vessel struck at about 7 a m. yesterday. The scene was witnessed from Glade House, and is represented to have been terrible. The sea ran mountains high, and as soon as she touched, the waves swept the unfortunate human beings upon her crowded decks by dozens into the sea. The spectators of this awful sight imagined that they could hear the cries of the victims as they were swept away, but as no boat, save the life-boat, could have lived in the gale, it was found impossible to render aid.

The life-boat left Cohasset early in the morning, and went to the aid of a British brig which was in danger at the mouth of the harbour, and carried her to a place of safety. They did not however visit the wreck, supposing that the long boat which they met going towards the shore, contained all that belonged to her.

When the St. John struck, her small boat was got ready, but was swamped at the side by the large number jumping into her. Shortly after the long boat broke her fastening, and floated off from the vessel. The captain and several others swam to and got on board of her, and landed in safety near Glade House. The second mate, two men and two boys of the crew were drowned.

After the ship struck the rocks, she thumped awhile, but shortly went to pieces, holding together not more than fifty or sixty minutes. Seven women and three men came ashore on pieces of the wreck, alive, but some very much exhausted. Two dead bodies were also taken from pieces of the wreck.

Early in the forenoon, the news of the wreck began to spread, and in the afternoon, the shore was lined with people who were active in getting bodies from the surf. Mr. Holmes, railroad conductor, was busy during the entire day in aiding the living and rescuing the dead bodies from the waves. One man, whose name we did not learn, came near losing his life in rescuing a body from the surf.

Towards nightfall the bodies began to come ashore and quite a number were taken from the surf, all, however, dead. Dead bodies were thrown upon the rocks, but before they could be rescued, the sea would carry them back again.

Quite a number of her passengers, especially women and children, were below when she struck, and were probably drowned there, as a hole was almost instantly thumped in her bottom. The long boat that reached the shore in safety contained, in addition to the captain and crew, only one passenger. Of the 7 first class passengers, who were all lost were three girls, nieces of the owner of the vessel. Great difficulty was experienced in saving those who came ashore on the pieces of the wreck, on account of the surf, which would throw them upon the rocks and then carry them to sea again. The poor creatures would cling with a death-grasp to the clothes of those who came to rescue them, and were with difficulty made to release their hold, even after having reached a place of safety.

One woman saved was very badly bruised upon the rocks, and it was thought last night that she would die, but she is this morning most comfortable.

It is stated that one passenger, clinging to a piece of a wreck, floated to the rocks, but was so far gone as to be unable to unclench his hand. Finally someone jumped on the fragment, made fast a rope to him, and he was got ashore. His face of a deep purple, his open mouth, fixed teeth, and deathly eyes, formed a sight long to be remembered.

So far only 26 dead bodies have been recovered, but the surf, which yet runs very high, is full of them. Before nightfall many more will doubtless be taken out. The shore is strewed with the baggage of the passengers all stove to pieces.

LATER ACCOUNTS
Capt. Oliver and his surviving mate reached this city at twelve o'clock. He states he made Cape Cod Light about 5 o'clock on Saturday evening, Scituate Light near 1 o'clock on Sunday morning; then stood away to the northward, to clear the land, for about three hours; then, it being about daylight, tacked ship and stood S.S.W., weather very thick; he came inside of Minot's Light House, and there saw a brig lying at anchor just inside of breakers, at a place called Hocksett Rock; tried to wear away up
to the brig, but found he could not fetch up, and threw over both anchors, which dragged; he then cut away her masts, and she drifted on to Grampus Ledge, where she went to pieces.

Previous to breaking up, the jolly-boat was hanging by the tackle, alongside, when the stern rigging bolt broke and the boat fell into the water. The captain, second mate, and two boys jumped in to get her clear, when about 25 passengers jumped in and swamped her. The twenty-five, together with second mate and two boys perished; the captain caught a rope hanging over the quarter, and was drawn on board by the first mate.

When the long boat was got clear a number of passengers jumped over to swim to her, but all perished. The captain, first mate (Mr. Crawford), and seven of the crew swam to and reached the boat.

The names of the drowned are probably unknown to the captain. He reports 120 souls on board, 21 of whom were saved, leaving 99 lost. The brig was in ballast.

All of the survivors were taken to Mr. Lathrop's house. They were chilled, bruised, and many of them senseless. Dr. Foster, the able and philanthropic physician of the village, attended them professionally, and it required untiring perseverance and skill to restore them. All but two of them are in a fair way of recovery. Mrs. Quinlan was struck upon the head with a very heavy piece of timber, which inflicted a severe wound, and she was otherwise both internally and externally injured. She will, however, speedily recover. Honora Burke is in a more critical situation. She was severely injured, and the struggle between life and death in her

case has been a severe one. She appears much better this morning, and were it not that she is likely to become a mother in a short time, the Doctor could speak confidentially in her case.

A watch was set all night on the beach, to rescue what bodies from the water that might be cast ashore. Mr. Lathrop, at whose house the survivors were taken, relates an incident that is at once touching and affecting. The waves were dashing high before him, and upon their crested tops, as they were breaking upon him, he saw what he thought was a small package of goods.

While watching to save even this small relic from the doomed vessel, it fell upon him striking upon his face. He reached forth his arm and grasped it - when, lo, he held an infant yet alive. He placed it in safety and that infant is now doing well in the family of a Mr. Gove, in this town.

From further conversation with the passengers and people of the town, it is certain to our mind, that Captain Oliver is liable to severe censure for some parts of his conduct. We would be the last to say one word the would add to the poignancy of his feelings in view of his great disaster; but, in a question involving the lives of more than one hundred fellow beings, we are bound to speak faithfully, the truth, as it has been presented to us.

It seems that on the afternoon of Saturday 6th inst., he numbered his passengers. Upwards of one hundred names were borne upon the manifest, or list, as two passengers called it who answered to the call. A line was then drawn across the deck, and between twenty and thirty other names were borne upon a small memorandum book. If the consignee has a duplicate list of passengers he or they should produce it. Unless a complete list can be produced we can never fully ascertain the exact number who perished on board this vessel on the fatal morning of October 9.

It is stated by three of the passengers that, on the afternoon of Saturday after they had made Provincetown Light, the Captain mustered his passengers on deck and joyfully assured them that the last night of their confinement on board had arrived.

A sad truth and most fearfully realized. His passage had been a good one and he felt elated. The simple and light-hearted passengers in the exuberance of their feelings prepared for an illumination; the deck and rigging were decorated with candles and dance and song wore away the evening of their LAST NIGHT ON BOARD THE ST. JOHN. The Captain dealt out his crew a treat of ardent spirits, and all on board participated in the joys and hopes incident to the termination of an Atlantic passage. Sad, sad, finale to their journey.

The following are the names of the few passengers who were saved:

- Captain Oliver
- Austin Kearin, age 20
- Catherine Flanagan, age 20
- Betsy Higgins, age 21
- Mary Keane, age 24
- Michael Fitzpatrick, age 26
- Michael Gibbon, age 26
- Barbara Kennelly, age 20

- Mary Slattery, age 20
- Michael Redding, age 24
- Honora Cullen,
- Honora Burke, age 27 (lost 3 children)
- Mrs. Quinlan.
- Mary Kane age 24 (lost 3 children)
- Peggy Adams
- Sally Sweeny

Information compiled from material supplied by Brud Slattery, Lahinch, John Flanagan, Lahinch and Frank Flanagan, suggests that there were only ninety-eight passengers and sixteen of a crew. Of the latter, nine men survived; five men and two boys died. Of the passengers, four men, eight women and one child reached the shore alive; twenty-three men, thirty-eight women and nineteen children were drowned. In all, ninety-two people lost their lives, not ninety-nine.

But this calculation assumes that the figure 90 for "steerage passengers lost" is in error; if it is correct, then the names of ten drowned were omitted at some stage.

Romantic Lighthouse
Minot Lighthouse's distinctive 1-4-3 (the number of letters in the phrase I Love You) white flash every thirty seconds has caused romantics to dub it the "I-Love-You" light earning it the title of the "Most Romantic Lighthouse" in the country. Situated two and a half miles from the shore, the lighthouse is visible for miles along the shore however best viewed by boat.

First Life Boat Station
In 1807 the Massachusetts Humane Society built its first lifeboat station in Cohasset, equipping it with a 30-foot, cork-lined whaleboat rowed by ten men. Many people would classify most of their rescue attempts as suicidal and many surf men died in the line of duty. Their motto, "You have to go out; you don't have to come back." However, rigorous training and tough equipment saw them through more often than not.

Theodore Parker Burbank

The Massachusetts Humane Society, modeled on Britain's Royal Humane Society, was established by an act of Congress in 1796. The Humane Society began by erecting Huts of Refuge, equipped with blankets, firewood, and food rations, along treacherous Massachusetts shorelines.

The Huts were positioned in locations that allowed shipwreck victims, who had made their way to shore, to aide in their own salvation and avoid dying of exposure. Early in the 1800s thirteen

The surfboat Nantucket

people froze to death on Lovell's Island after surviving a shipwreck.

Station Stats
Station Established: 1850
Current Tower First Lit: 1860   Automated: 1947
Foundation Materials: Stone Ledge
Construction Materials: Granite
Tower Shape: Conical
Markings/Pattern: Natural
Original Lens: Third Order, Fresnel 1860

Plymouth Light (Gurnet Light)

Haunted Light and Sand Bar

The present day Gurnet Light is a thirty-four foot white octagonal wooden tower accessible to residents only using a four-wheel-drive vehicle from Duxbury Beach. Its light flashes three times every 30 seconds with a red sector, a fourth order Fresnel; its fog signal is one blast every 15 seconds. It is not open to the public.

The Gurnet Point Light is located at the distant entrance to Plymouth Harbor overlooking where the Pilgrims came ashore in 1620 and is one of America's earliest lighthouses being the eighth light built in the Colonies. The Pilgrims named the point "the gurnett's nose" reportedly after the fish of that name which is caught off the coast of England.

Hanna Haunts the Lighthouse

John Thomas was the first Keeper and his wife Hanna was the first woman to become Lighthouse keeper after her husband's death at the Battle of Quebec. It's believed that Hannah still on duty at the light. A couple that spent a night at the Lighthouse is reported as saying:

Something woke Bob. He rose up on his elbow and watched the light come around, illuminating the windows for a few seconds each time. Then he looked over toward me and saw the head and shoulders of a woman floating

111

above my bed. He described her as having a green blue electric spark color. He said she had an old time hairdo, sunken cheeks and the saddest face he ever saw. Bob told me that she wasn't wrinkled and he didn't think she was an old woman. He said he felt no threat from her, but only her sadness. As he watched her, out of the corner of his eye he could see the rays of light from the lighthouse come around several times, brightening the room. He looked toward the light, looked back to where she had been and she was gone.

America's first woman lighthouse keeper apparently is still on the job.

Christmas Eve Tragedy – 1778

It was Christmas 1778, and heavy snow was falling upon Boston Harbor. The brigantine *General Arnold*, named for the gallant hero of Quebec, was at anchor off Nantasket Road in Boston Harbor. At the break of dawn, she set sail for the Carolinas, alongside the privateer *Revenge*.

The *Arnold* carried 21 guns, a detachment of Marines, and a cargo of military supplies for the American troops who were attempting to stop the British from cutting off the South from the Northern

Winter storm *lashes grounded ship*

colonies. Her commander was Captain James Magee, an Irish born American patriot, who was looking forward to meeting up with the British, his lifelong enemy. Before the day was over, however, he would lose his ship to a greater enemy, the enraged sea.

Of the 105 men and boys who sailed with him, 81 would die a horrible death, and the others, all but himself, would be crippled for life. Under full sail, the two privateers headed across

Massachusetts Bay toward the open sea. The wind picked up, the snow fell harder, and soon they were in the midst of a Nor'East blizzard. Captain Barrows of the *Revenge* decided to ride out the storm offshore of Cape Cod. Magee felt that his ship could weather the storm better in Plymouth Harbor behind Gurnet Point. But, the Arnold's anchor wouldn't hold, and she began to drift into the long harbor.

Magee had his men dismount 16 of the deck cannons and store them below to add weight to the hull and give the vessel stability. Her sails were furled and to the topmost struck, but nothing seemed to stop The *Arnold's* dragging anchor. Huge waves broke over the bow and quickly turned to ice adding more weight to the stricken ship.

The anchor cable broke and the *Arnold* sailed backwards into the harbor, bumped over a sand bar (Brown's Bank), and scraped to a sudden stop on top of shallow water sand flat, only a mile from shore.

At first, Magee and his men thought they could lighten the vessel and slide her over the flat to shore. With axes, they cut down her masts, but the heavy hull was already sinking into the sand, cracking her boards and leaking salt water into her hold. Icy waves washed over her main deck and the captain later reported "The quarter deck was the only place that could afford the most distant prospect of safety." Magee went on to say "Within a few hours, presented a scene that would shock the least delicate humanity. Some of my people were stifled to death with the snow, others perished with the extremity of the cold, and a few were washed off the deck and drowned."

There were a few bottles and casks of wine and brandy in the cargo. Some of the crew members ventured below into the half flooded hold to drown themselves in liquid warmth. Some were drunk before Captain Magee realized they had broken into the stores. He pleaded with them to pour the brandy into their shoes to prevent frostbite, instead of drinking it. Some obeyed, but those who did not were dead by the next morning.

Those huddled together on the quarterdeck, their clothes first drenched then frozen to their bodies, covered themselves with the sails for protection from the salt spray and the snow. By the morning of the 26th, thirty of them were frozen to death. The blizzard continued. Magee could see but a shadow of land through the falling snow, so he fired his signal gun in hopes of getting the attention of the people of the town. Three crewmen managed to launch the privateers long boat into the wild sea, then started rowing to shore, but they were lost sight of and never heard from again.

Late in the afternoon when there was a short break in the storm, the people of Plymouth sent dories out from shore, however, none of them could make it to the stranded vessel. They decided that the only way to the *Arnold* was to build a causeway of ice and snow one mile long out to the sand flat. Working throughout the night, through the next day and night, the people of Plymouth accomplished what seemed impossible - they built a road out to the distressed privateer.

Meanwhile the shipwreck victims spent a second and third night on the quarter-deck in sub-freezing temperatures. The living feared going to sleep, knowing that if they did, they probably would not wake up again. In an attempt to block out wind and waves, they piled the dead bodies of their comrades around them. The *Arnold* sank deeper into the sand, knee deep water now covering the main deck. In an effort to keep his remaining crewmen and Marines alive, Captain Magee requested, and then demanded, that the men keep walking around and exercising on the little deck in order to maintain their circulation.

He was especially anxious about two boys aboard: Connie Marchang, age 10 and Barney Downs, age 15. Magee prodded them to walk in place even though they were both so exhausted and frozen they could hardly stand. He urged them over and over again not to give up. Marchant later said, "I ascribe my preservation mainly to the reiterated efforts of Captain Magee."

On Monday morning, December 28th when the causeway was completed, the people of Plymouth passed over the ice to the wreck. "It was a scene unutterably awful and distressing", writes

Plymouth's Doctor Thatcher. "The ship was sunk ten feet in the sand; the waves had been for about thirty six hours sweeping the main deck, and even here they were obliged to pile together dead bodies to make room for the living. Seventy dead bodies, frozen in to all imaginable postures, were strewn over the deck, or attached to shrouds and spars; about thirty exhibited signs of life, but were unconscious whether in life or death.

The bodies remained in the posture in which they died, the features dreadfully distorted. Some were erect, some bending forward, some sitting with the head resting on the knees, and some with both arms extended, clinging to spars or some part of the vessel." Sleds and slabs of wood were used to carry the survivors and the stiffened corpses over the ice road to shore. The dead were piled in the Plymouth Courthouse, the living brought to local homes to spend agonizing hours thawing out."

Magee skippered merchant ships out of Salem for the remainder of his life, including the famous *Astrea* that opened American trade with China. Whenever in homeport at Christmas, Magee called for a reunion of the 24 *Arnold* survivors, assisting any who were destitute with a gift from his own wages. At his request, when he died, he was buried with the *Arnold* crew at Burial Hill, Plymouth, MA.

Plymouth's Burial Hill monument memorializes the tragedy

The Ghosts of Brown's Bank

Brown's Bank, the location of the horrific tragedy of Christmas Eve 1778, is apparently still haunted by the souls that perished here hundreds of years ago. Not many people find themselves in a situation to experience these spirits as Brown's Bank is in the ocean and far from shore.

Few venture onto the bank during daytime and even fewer at night in a thick fog. However, one couple was returning to Marshfield in their boat after spending the evening at one of Plymouth's fine waterfront restaurants where they celebrated their wedding anniversary.

The husband recounts the event: *We rounded the Bug Light and headed out towards the Gurnet when we ran into a low-lying fog bank. We were not*

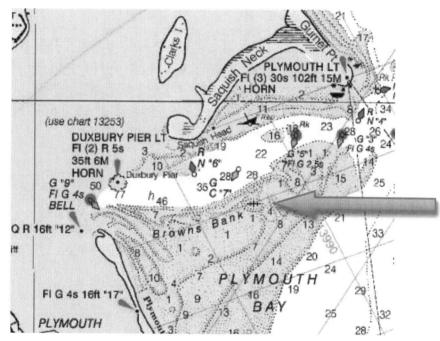

Chart showing Brown's Bank and the wreck of the *Arnold's* location

concerned as we were very familiar with the waters and plotted a compass course that would bring us to the Number 2 buoy and the open sea. All was proceeding as planned when we heard music playing, it sounded close by. Where was it coming from?

Assuming the only source must be from the rocky shores and a party at a Saquish Neck cottage. I turned the boat hard right so as to avoid the shore. The next thing I know my wife shouts - Look out! It was low tide and we had come onto Brown's Bank. It happened so quickly that it was obvious we

116

couldn't have been close to the Saquish Neck shore. But then, where was the music coming from?

Suddenly, above the low hanging fog we saw it; the returning Plymouth to Provincetown Ferry having a party, it was their music we were hearing. The boat passed and the fog began to lift so we were off Brown's Bank and heading home to Marshfield. My wife was very quiet the whole way back and after we were safely on shore I asked why she was so silent.

Her reply – Brown's Bank is haunted! I had an overwhelming feeling of doom and sadness that was so deep I felt I couldn't speak. I recognized the feeling as being exactly what I experienced when we were at Gettysburg where so many died in battle. The spirits of those poor souls lost in such awful conditions linger still and so do the frozen men from the "Arnold."

History

The area surrounding the light known as Gurnet Point and Saquish Neck was occupied seasonally for thousands of years before Europeans arrived by the Womponoag Tribe. The Tribe lived throuout eastern Massachusetts and the Islands of Martha's Vineyard and Nantucket and would spend their summers here to avoid the heat and mesquitoes found inland. Saquish is a Wompanoag word meaning "Place of many clams".

In 1004 it is said, the ship of Eric the Red's son Thorwald was damaged off Cape Cod. Putting into shore for repairs to the keel, the ship was attacked by natives, and Thorwald was mortally wounded. After completing repairs, Thorwald and his crew sailed into a large bay and landed at the foot of a hilly, heavily-wooded promontory (Gurnet Point). Tradition has it that Thorwald proclaimed at that spot, "It is beautiful here, I should like to affix my abode." Not long after this Thorwald died from the wounds he suffered in the skirmish with the Indians. His men buried him on Gurnet Point.

1605 - Before the arrival of the Pilgrims in 1620, both John Smith and Samuel de Champlain had written about the area. Champlain described the Gurnet in 1605 as practically an island covered principally with pine trees. He is said to have marveled at the ability of the Indians to catch cod with fishhooks made of wood or bone that were attached to the end of a spear.

The 1710 "Light" Replaced - 1768

The Massachusetts Legislature authorized the construction of a Lighthouse in 1768 to replace a primitive Light structure erected in 1710. The structure is thought to have been Lanterns raised on poles, as early records do not refer to any type of structure having been erected.

The new lighthouse was built on the high bluff at the end of the long peninsula known as Duxbury Beach and completed in 1769 at a cost of 660 pounds. This structure consisted of a house with two lantern rooms on the roof 20 feet high, one at each end. This was the first twin-lighthouse constructed in America.

The First Keeper

The first keeper was John Thomas on whose land the original lighthouse was built, and for which rent of 5 shillings per year was paid him by the colony. John served as a physician in the French and Indian war and in 1775 raised a regiment of volunteers for the Revolutionary War with Britain and subsequently was appointed as brigadier general. It was the practice in the day that the landowner was appointed as the keeper.

While he was away, which appears to be most of the time, his wife Hannah attended the light. She decided to extinguish it 1776, as it was becoming an aid to British war ships attacking unarmed American merchant shipping off the Plymouth coast.

Lighthouse Hit by British Cannonball - 1775

During the Revolution, the three towns of Plymouth, Duxbury, and Kingston had erected an earthen fort, Fort Standish, on the Gurnet. In the midst of an engagement between the Fort and the British frigate *Niger*, which had gone aground on Brown's Bank, a shot from the ship hit the lighthouse blowing a hole in its side. Later, a rising tide floated the vessel off the sand bar and it escaped. The Gurnet Light is the only United States lighthouse to ever have been engaged in a battle and been the casualty of a cannon ball strike.

First Woman Lighthouse Keeper

In 1776 George Washington promoted John Thomas to major general and was dispatched to Canada and the Battle of Quebec where he subsequently died of smallpox on June 2, 1776. The General Assembly replaced Hannah, his widow as the first woman light keeper in America. It is reported that her ghost still awaits her husband's return from the war in which he died so many years ago.

Lighthouse Destroyed by Fire - 1801

On July 2, 1801, the lighthouse was completely destroyed by fire. The merchants of Plymouth and Duxbury erected a temporary beacon at their own expense. On April 6, 1802, Congress appropriated $270 to reimburse them. At the same time Congress also appropriated $2,500 "for rebuilding the lighthouse on Gurnet." Twin lights were built and the Thomas family was paid $120 for the land on which the new two lighthouses were constructed.

Twin Lights Built - 1802

Records reveal - "They require being double to distinguish them from the single light at Barnstable. They are in separate towers, 22 feet high and 30 feet apart they consist of a single series of six lamps each, with old 8 1/2-inch reflectors, arranged in a circular form, so as to suit the harbor as well as sea navigation. Their elevation is 70 feet

Postcard showing the twin Lights

above the level of the sea, enabling them to be seen 19 miles."

In 1842 North America's first "twin lights", the Gurnet lighthouses. were rebuilt and the new structures, while still of wood, each had a distinctive design. In 1871 the lights were of the sixth order and were declared by the Lighthouse Board to be "entirely too small" and "readily mistaken for the lights in a dwelling house, when they can be seen at all." Their distance apart was also too short to afford an efficient distinction."

In 1924 the northeast tower was discontinued and the station is now described as a white, octagonal, pyramidal tower, with white dwelling, 39 feet above ground and 102 feet above water. Its 700,000 candlepower, fourth-order electric light shows group flashing white every 20 seconds and is visible for 16 miles. An air diaphragm horn blasts for 3 seconds every 15 seconds during fog.

In 1986 the light was automated, with a modern optic replacing the Fresnel lens. Plymouth Light continues to serve as an active aid to navigation with a flashing white light and a red sector warning vessels away from the Mary Ann Rocks.

US Coast Guard Photos

In the late 1980s - Plymouth Light was leased by the Coast Guard to the Massachusetts Chapter of the U.S. Lighthouse Society. Volunteers lived in the adjacent keeper's house, and the property was open to overnight visitors. The lease later reverted back to the Coast Guard.

1998 the lighthouse, now only 50' from the cliff's edge, was moved back from the eroding cliff approximately 140 feet onto the Fort Standish site.

Scituate Lighthouse

Army of Two, Ghosts and Shipwrecks

Heroines Haunt the Lighthouse

Simeon Bates, the first keeper of the Light, was the father of nine children. Two of his teenage daughters were destined to become famous figures in Colonial America's history.

British raids on coastal New England towns were frequent during the War of 1812. So it was not surprising when in September of 1812, while Keeper Bates and his family were in town, leaving teenage daughters Rebecca and Abigail in charge while they were gone, such an attack began to unfold.

Seeing the British frigate *H.M.S. Bulwark*, anchor close to shore not far from the Lighthouse the two sisters immediately hatched a very clever plan to save the town from attack. As the British lowered small boats and began rowing ashore the sisters grabbed their fife and drum, hid behind some thick shrubs so as not to be seen, and began to loudly play a marching tune.

The British believed the music signaled the approach of the town's militia. Because they were in a vulnerable position while aboard their small rowboats, they wisely turned around, returned to their ship and sailed away. The sisters had saved the town from attack with their clever plan.

The sisters in fact did become famous figures in America's history and, shortly before their deaths; Congress awarded the Bates sisters pensions in recognition of their bravery and heroism.

Many claim the spirits of Rebecca and Abigail Bates still haunt the lighthouse. It is claimed by many that they have heard fife and drum music coming from Cedar Point near the lighthouse.

The *Etrusco* on the beach at Cedar Point in 1956

Shipwrecks On and Off Scituate Lighthouse

Beginning in 1807 and up to 1919 nearly one hundred significant shipwrecks had been recorded on and along the Scituate cost. No one knows the number of less significant yet still important lives and vessels lost.

Perhaps the most famous shipwreck at Scituate Lighthouse occurred during a blizzard on March 16, 1956 when the Italian freighter *Etrusco* ran aground only yards from the lighthouse. The Coast Guard, using breeches buoy, rescued the entire crew. Nine

months later it was floated off at high tide
after tons of rock had been blasted away
freeing the ship from the grasp of the shore.
Thousands of the curious made their way to
Scituate to see and take pictures of the
enormous ship right on the beach.

Fiery Shipwreck off Scituate
On January 10, 1930 the tanker *Pinthis*,
carrying a cargo of 12,000 barrels of oil, collided with the liner *Faifax*
in a fog about six miles off Scituate's Fourth Cliff. The tanker
exploded, capsized and sank in less than twenty minutes. All 19 of
her crew were lost. The sea burned for several days following the
sinking from the escaping oil. The *Fairfax* caught fire and many of
her crew were injured or burned to death. Forty-seven people lost
their lives in this tragedy.

Two Ships Down in the "Portland Storm" of 1898
The barge *Delaware* sank off Collamore Ledge and the pilot schooner
Columbia both were lost on November 26, 1898. All hands on both

The pilot schooner *Columbia* on the beach near Scituate Light 1898

vessels were lost to the sea; only three bodies of the estimated dozen
lost were ever recovered.

Treasure off Scituate

The full rigged cargo vessel *Forest Queen* went down in a violent storm, February 29, 1853 mere yards off Scituate's Second Cliff Beach while carrying twelve tons of silver ingots. Much has been recovered and the state has granted salvage rights to a private party.

Occasional, a seventy-three lb bar of silver has been known to wash up onto the shore during strong surf and storms. How many bars have been buried under the sands of Scituate

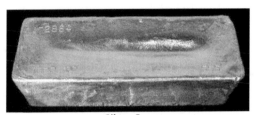

Silver Ingot

beaches and are yet to be uncovered? Metal detector anyone?

More Shipwrecks off Scituate

1807 Scituate-built *Cordelia,* returning from China piled up on a ledge within the sight of where she was built.

1919 the bark *Professor Koch* with a two million dollar cargo of hides and wool from South Africa crashed on the rocks near Cedar Point.

1926 the Schooner *Kenwood,* built at the McKie Shipbuilding Co in East Boston, was blown onto the rocks on the north side of Cedar Point during a February Blizzard. The eight crewmen all survived.

1930 the *Southland* a 205' wooden steamer built in 1917 as a troop carrier during WWI sank off Scituate during a storm on December 2, 1930.

History

By 1810 Scituate, Massachusetts had flourished becoming a major fishing port. The entrance to its protective harbor was difficult, especially after dark, because of the shallow water and narrow channel at the entrance. Congress appropriated $4,000 for the construction of the eleventh lighthouse in the new nation. The twenty-five foot tall light, located on Cedar Point, was lit in September 1811, two months ahead of schedule.

By 1810 Scituate, Massachusetts had flourished becoming a major fishing port. The entrance to its protective harbor was difficult, especially after dark, because of the shallow water and narrow channel at the entrance. Congress appropriated $4,000 for the construction of the eleventh lighthouse in the new nation. The twenty-five foot tall light, located on Cedar Point, was lit in September 1811, two months ahead of schedule.

By 1841 in an attempt to abate the continuous loss of shipping on Minots Ledge which lay a few miles away and further to sea, a more powerful lighting apparatus was installed and the tower raised to forty feet to increase its visibility at sea.

On Again, Off Again
Upon completion of Minots Ledge Light in 1850 Scituate Light went dark, as it no longer was required. However, the first Minot's Ledge Light was destroyed in an April 1852 storm and so Scituate Light was pressed back into service. The lighthouse received a new Fresnel lens in 1855. When the second Minots Ledge Light was relit in 1860, Scituate Light was extinguished, seemingly forever

In 1890 Congress authorized the funds to construct a 630-foot breakwater off the end of Cedar Point. A year later in 1891 a small iron frame tower and light was erected at the end of the jetty. The light was fueled by kerosene and shone a steady red beam thirty-one feet above sea level. Since 1958 this light has been electrified. In 1991 Scituate Lighthouse was relit but the light can only be seen from land.

Town Acquires the Lighthouse

In 1916 the Town of Scituate purchased the lighthouse from the federal government for $1000. In 1930 the Town, at the height of the Depression, built a new lantern room atop the light. The justification; *"a community is judged by the condition of its public buildings; therefore the lighthouse should be well kept and in pleasing looking condition."*

The 1968 Town Meeting awarded custody and administration of the Lighthouse to the Scituate Historical Society. In 2001 the Scituate Historical Society completed the Scituate Lighthouse Runway Exhibit, more than twenty graphic panels on the history of the lighthouse lining the walkway from the house to the tower.

Station Stats

Station Established: 1811
First Lit: 1811
Deactivated: 1860-1994
Foundation Materials: Natural/Emplaced
Construction Materials: Granite/Brick
Height: 25 feet
Tower Shape: Octagonal
Markings/Pattern: Solid White with Green Lantern Room Roof
Characteristics: White over red light
Original Lens: Pan Lamp 1811; Fresnel lens in 1855

Nauset Light

Located on an Outer Cape Bluff
Haunted by a Famous Ghost

Nauset Light, or, as it is known officially, Nauset Beach Light, is made of a cast iron plate shell lined with brick and stands 48 feet high on a bluff in the town of Eastham on Cape Cod. Its light, alternating red and white flashes every five seconds. You might recognize the lighthouse as the logo of the Cape Cod Potato Chips Co.

It was added to the National Register of Historic Places in 1987 as Nauset Beach Light. Nauset Light was originally constructed in the nearby town of Chatham in 1877 and was one of two lights. It was moved to Eastham in 1923 to replace the "Three Sisters of Nauset", three small wood lighthouses that had been decommissioned. The light was automated and the keeper's house sold in 1955.

Due to coastal erosion, by the early 1990s Nauset Light was less than 50 feet from the edge of the 70-foot cliff on which it stood. In 1993, the Coast Guard proposed decommissioning the light. Following a great public outcry, the non-profit Nauset Light Preservation Society was formed and funded, and in 1995, it leased the lighthouse from the Coast Guard. The organization arranged for the light to be relocated, in November 1996, to a location 336 feet west of its original position. The move occurred none too soon as the lighthouse, by then, was only 37 feet from the cliff's edge.

Area Haunted by the Ghost of a Pirate's Lover

Many visitors and residents alike have reported seeing what is thought to be the ghost of "Goody Hallett", the teenage lover of the pirate Black Sam Bellamy.

Fishermen on Nauset Light Beach have reported seeing a woman constantly shaking a blanket and, when approached, she disappears. "Goody's" ghost has been appearing to the unsuspecting on the Outer Cape since the early 1700's.

Black Sam Bellamy was an adventurer who left his wife and family in England to search the Caribbean and locate at least one of the

Maria "Goody" Hallett

nearly one hundred gold and treasure laden Spanish Galleons that were destroyed in a massive hurricane several decades earlier.

He stopped at Cape Cod on his way and it was here that young Sam Bellamy met and seduced the very beautiful Eastham farm girl, Maria Hallett, in the spring of 1716.

By all accounts Sam Bellamy was a rouge and a simple, blustering windbag of a man. His adventuresome spirit and gift of gab had enabled him to finance his quest for gold and also to seduce the loveliest girl on Cape Cod, Maria Hallett.

The Saga of Maria "Goody" Hallett

Maria was a naïve fifteen-year-old farm girl from a well respected, church going Eastham family. The handsome sailor's sweet talk and tales of treasure and adventure impressed the wide-eyed Maria. He convinced her that he would marry her when he returned laden with silver, gold and jewels that he would recover from sunken treasure ships in the Caribbean. As fall approached and the days shortened and grew cooler, he sailed south to begin his great adventure.

That winter Maria was found lying in a cold Eastham barn with her dead baby in her arms. She was at once taken into town and attached to deacon Doane's whipping post and given several lashes before being thrown into jail. The selectmen spoke of charging her with murder. They said she must be made an example to others of the godless younger generation of the day.

It seemed that no cell could contain the young lass, and she continually escaped to wander the shore calling out the name of her lost love. Eastham gave up its attempts to keep her in jail and released the young girl upon the condition she would leave town and never return.

She made her home in a shack in the dunes of Cape Cod's outer shore and eked out a living by doing menial jobs. In short order, the once most beautiful girl in Eastham had become haggard and worn and

Was "Goody" really a witch?

unrecognizable to those who had known her before Bellamy.

Maria Labeled a Witch, Given the Name "Goody"

Townspeople were convinced that she was a witch, and they now referred to as "Goody" Hallett. The name Goody, as defined in the American College Dictionary, was "a polite term applied to a woman in humble life."

Goody must have been extremely depressed and traumatized experiencing the death of her baby. Then to be shunned by friends and family, jailed then driven out of town combined, causing her to lose her mind.

All of this happened in the era of the famous Salem witch trials so it was in keeping with the times for the town folks to condemn her as a witch, a person who had sold her soul to the devil. Goody would continually be seen walking the high Outer Cape cliffs gazing out to sea screaming curses into the winds on even the stormiest of winter nights. Even today her ghost is said to walk the seaside cliffs of Cape Cod's outer shore and along the beaches near where Captain Black Bellamy's treasure ship, the *Whydah*, went down on April 26, 1717.

Could Goody Conjure up Storms

Could witch Goody have had a hand in brewing storms that shipwrecked more than two thousand ships and drowned uncounted thousands of mariners, including her lover captain Black Sam Bellamy, on the sandbars off the Outer Cape? There are those who believe she did.

Lynne McIlveen Illustration

Goody swallowed by a whale

On that fateful day in April 1717, at the height of a fierce storm, as the *Whydah* was sinking and sailors were drowning in the raging surf people on the beach say they saw her high on the cliff shrieking thanks to the Devil for vengeance. All this happened on the Outer Cape sand dunes near the lonely dilapidated shack in which Goody lived.

Goody Swallowed by a Whale?

Goody's life came to a dramatic end on April 22, 1751 when she was reportedly swallowed by a whale. This tale's veracity is supported by the fact that when a whale was cut open, inside they found Maria's red slippers. Other tales have Goody riding upon the backs of whales with lanterns affixed to their tails in order to lure unsuspecting mariners onto the reefs and shoals of the outer cape referred to at the time as the "Graveyard of the Atlantic". She is also supposed to have the power, as she was a witch, to conjure up storms and gales to the peril of seamen of the day; Storms such as the one that sank the *Whydah* and sent her scallywag lover to Davy Jones' locker.

Her Lover's Treasure Ship Sinks off Outer Cape Beach

On April 26, off Cape Cod, the *Whydah* and its crew of 148 souls ran into an intense late winter storm. Despite Herculean efforts of the crew, the *Whydah* struck the bar off a beach in what is now the Cape Cod National Seashore Park and sank as raging surf tore her to pieces.

People along the beach watching the tragic scene reported seeing "Goody" Hallett high upon the bluff screaming thanks to the Devil for vengeance. The next day a search for survivors and perhaps treasure revealed only bits and pieces of floating remains of the once proud flagship *Whydah* and her crew.

Of the eight that survived the wreck six were jailed, tried as pirates and hung on the gallows. Only two lived to tell the stories of Captain Black Sam Bellamy: an Indian pilot and Thomas Davis, a Welsh carpenter. Nothing is known of what became of the pilot but it was Davis' vivid account of the shipwreck that was passed from generation to generation.

In 1984, Cape Cod native Barry Clifford discovered the wreckage of the *Whydah* in the shallow waters off of the Outer Cape. The value of the treasure is estimated to be in the multi millions.

Race Point Light

Marks beginning of the "Graveyard of the Atlantic" and is home to a flag waving ghost.

Race Point Light

Race Point Light is located at the v ery tip of Cape Cod. On a sunny summer day it is almost impossible to imagine the death and destruction that has occurred off its shore. The Old Harbor Lifesaving Station located on the beach nearby should lend a clue.

Graveyard of the Atlantic
The stretch of the Cape Cod coast from Race Point to Monomoy Island was infamously known as the *Graveyard of the Atlantic*. At least four ships a month were lost here until the opening of the Cape Cod Canal in 1914. More than three thousand s ships were lost and many more thousands of mariners drowned.

In fact there were so many shipwrecks here that an industry evolved to salvaged the ships and debris (flotsam and jetsam) washed up on the beach. A small fishing village named "Helltown" was established near Race Point at Herring Cove that allegedly headquartered "Mooncussers." These rouges would use moonless nights to lure ships to their destruction by hanging false lights on poles to simulate navigation beacons.

Why is this Beautiful Coast so Deadly?

In a northeast blow, ships would enter the trough of Peaked Hill Bar with the wind behind them and not be able to tack or navigate out of the deadly triangle. Others, being a mile or more at sea, were surprised to find themselves in a beach like surf and then, aground on the shifting sand of Peaked Hill Bar.

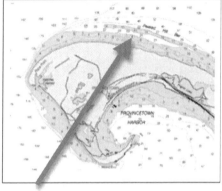

Peaked Hill Bar

The chart shows the shallow water extending far out into the Atlantic with a trough of deep water and then the shallows of Peaked Hill Bar.

Patriotic Ghost?

One might wonder how Race Point could not be haunted with so many unfortunates having lost their lives off its shore. There is a ghostly tale recounted by a former president of the Cape Cod Chapter of the American Lighthouse Foundation.

It is reported that an unknown entity keeps replacing American flags that had been tattered by wind and storms. Unexplainably, every time a flag became damaged or shredded in a storm, a new one would replace it. It is unknown the origin of the ghost; perhaps a patriotic mariner lost in one of the many shipwrecks off Race Point.

Want to Spend a Few Nights at the Lighthouse?

The Cape Cod Chapter of the American Lighthouse Foundation's dedicated volunteer maintains the lighthouse and rent it and the Keeper's house, the Whistle house, the Oil house from May through October.

You can make reservations by telephone 855-722-3959 or from the Foundation's website http://www.mybnbwebsite.com/racepointlighthouse.

Race Point History

The Light was first established in 1816, the third light on Cape Cod (after Highland Light (1797) and Chatham Light (1808)). The original light was a 25 feet rubble stone tower that featured one of the earliest rotating beacons, which distinguished it from others on Cape Cod.

In 1858 the light got a fourth order Fresnel lens and, in 1874, a second keeper's quarters. In 1875, after significant deterioration of the original tower, it was replaced with an iron tower lined with brick. The original keeper's house was rebuilt as part of this project. The station was electrified in 1957. The larger keeper's house was removed in 1960 and the other was updated.

Lighthouse Stats

Year first constructed	November 1816
Year first lit	1876 (current structure)
Automated	1972
Foundation	Natural/emplaced
Construction	Iron plate with brick interior
Tower shape	Conical
Markings / pattern	White with black lantern
Height	45 feet
Focal height	41 feet above mean sea level
Original lens	Fourth-order Fresnel lens
Current lens	Solar powered VRB-25
Flash	Flashing White every 10 seconds
Fog horn	Two blasts every 60 seconds
Range	16 nautical miles (18 mi)

Wolf Howling at the Moon

Maine and New Hampshire

Haunted Lighthouses, Ships and Forts

New Hampshire:
> Portsmouth Harbor Lighthouse
> Fort Constitution a/k/a Fort William & Mary

South Coast
> Cape Neddick Light
> Boon Island Light
> Ghost Ship of Harswell
> Wood Island Light
> Ram Island Light
> Portland Head Light

Mid Coast
> Hendrick Light
> Marshall Point Light
> Manticus Light
> Fort William Henry
> Pemaquid Point Light
> Sequin Island Light
> Owl's Head Light
> Fort Knox

Bold Coast
> Mount Desert Light
> Prospect Harbor Light
> Winter Harbor Light
> West Quody Light

New Hampshire

Arial view of Portsmouth Harbor Lighthouse and Fort
Constitution a/k/a Fort William and Mary

Portsmouth Harbor Lighthouse -
Fort Constitution formerly Fort William and Mary

Ghost of the 1874 Keeper Still on the Job

Portsmouth Harbor lighthouse was built in 1771 on the island of
New Castle at the mouth of the Pistatgua River. It is built at the
location first fortified by the British in the early 1600's and on the
grounds of what was once Fort William and Mary. The British
occupied it until the end of the American Revolution. After the
colonialists won the Revolution the fort was renamed Fort
Constitution. The conical structure is 48 ft tall; the Light fixed
green; Present optic: Fourth-order Fresnel; visible 12 nautical miles;
Fog signal one blast every 10 seconds.

Children Haunt the Fort
On July 4, 1809 gunpowder, stored for use in a Fourth of July
fireworks display, accidentally exploded killing 14 people, most of
whom were children. Many believe it is the victims of the 1809
explosion that haunt the structure today. Many a tourist has claimed
to take photos, while in the fort, that were obscured by
unexplainable green smoke. Many Coast Guardsmen are said to be
afraid to go into Fort Constitution at night because of the eerie

noises they hear and the uneasiness they feel. It is reported that almost everyone who enters the fort says they experience a very heavy feeling in their chest while walking through the fort's passageways.

Ghost of Keeper Joshua Card

Joshua Card was a man of the sea. His father was a mariner and Joshua would follow him to sea at the age of twelve serving as a cabin boy aboard a schooner. At the age of 27 he gave up the sea going life, married and began a family. After a few years working in Portsmouth he spent the next forty-one years as a lighthouse keeper; six years at Boon Island Light and thirty-five years at Portsmouth Harbor Light. He retired, against his will, at age 87 as the seacoast's oldest lighthouse keeper and died two years later. Many believe he refused to retire and is on the job even today as the "Ghostly Keeper" at Portsmouth Harbor Light.

Coast Guard personnel stationed nearby at the fort often sight a "shadowy figure" floating about the grounds at night. Workers at the lighthouse have heard voices and seen apparitions resembling a keeper wearing an old fashion uniform.

New England's Haunted Lighthouses and more

Haunted Keeper's Quarters

The Keeper's Quarters, nestled within the granite walls of the Fort Constitution, are now the Coast Guard Station. Many believe Joshua's spirit still resides in his former home. Visitors report hearing footsteps in the house and the sound of a fan emanating from what used to be Joshua's bedroom.

Ghostly Keeper on TV

In October 2008 ghost seekers from the program "Ghost Hunters" came to investigate, film, and perhaps explain the strange activities surrounding the fort and lighthouse. They investigated and videotaped all night inside the Lighthouse, the Fort, and the Keeper's Quarters. They obtained some interesting evidence.

Most of the paranormal activity occurred inside the lighthouse. Two teams heard the sounds of footsteps walking on the stairway. Two team members communicated with whatever was making the noises by knocking on the wall, with the entity responding back. Proof of the knocking response and footsteps were recorded on video. In the basement of the keeper's quarters the team heard voices and a slamming of a door, all captured on tape.

Joshua Card was said to be a good-humored man who loved his work seldom leaving the lighthouse he apparently still calls home.

Station Stats

Station Established: 1771
Present Tower Built: 1878
Automated: 1960
Construction Material: Cast iron with brick lining
Tower Height: 48 feet
Focal Plane: 52 feet
Present optic: Fourth-order Fresnel lens
Characteristic: Fixed Green; Visibility: 12 nautical miles
Fog signal: Mariner Radio Activated Sound Signal (MRASS), one blast every 10 seconds

EDW.^D KELLY, A MAGICIAN.
in the act of invoking the Spirit of a Deceased Person

Maine

South Coast

Mooncussers at Work

Cape Neddick Light, a/k/a Nubble Light

Seven Coffins, Phantom Sailors and a Ghost Ship

Ghost Ship Sails into Eternity

On morning of Wednesday, November 30th 1842 the three masted bark Isadore, a beautiful vessel of four hundred tons burden, commanded and owned by Capt. Leander Foss set sail for New Orleans on its maiden voyage.

Shortly after setting sail the weather turned foul; the wind increased to near hurricane force with a blinding heavy wet snow. The ship was driven onto the rocks on a point of rocks near Cape Neddick, called Bald Head, and wrecked. The entire crew of fifteen perished.

Fateful Premonition

Before it sailed on its first and fateful voyage, a sailor dreamt of seven coffins lined up on shore and an unworldly voice told him that one would be his. A second crewmember, Thomas King, also dreamt of the wreck. The dream was so real and so frightened him that King hid on shore until after the Isadore had sailed.

Soon seven bodies (including that of the prophetic seaman), washed ashore, followed by the captain's leg; the rest of his body was never found. The crew, ranged in age from the 15 year-old cabin boy to the 53-year old cook, all hailed from the Kennebunk, Maine area. A gravestone was erected in the cemetery at Kennebunkport to memorialize Captain Leander Foss and the tragedy.

Still Sailing the Maine Coast

Some say the Isadore, the phantom ship of the Maine coast, with its crew can still be seen sailing past Cape Neddick Light and elsewhere along Maine's rocky shores.

One day at dusk an Isle of Shoals fisherman saw a bark close-reefed, with shadowy men in dripping cloths who stared straight ahead from their stations on the bark. He and many others believe the bark is still on its maiden voyage sailing the seas with its phantom crew.

History

Cape Neddick Lighthouse is located on Nubble Island 100 yards off Cape Neddick Point, York, Maine. In 1602 explorer Bartholomew Gosnold met with local Indians on the island and dubbed it "Savage Rock."

A letter describing Bartholomew's encounter with Natives on Savage Rock as described by historian John Brereton: *The fourteenth of May, 1602, about six in the morning we decried land that we called Savage Rock, because the savages first showed themselves there... whom we supposed at first to be Christians distressed. They came bold aboard us, being all naked, saving about their shoulder certain loose deer skins, and near their wastes seal skins tied fast like Irish dimmie trowsers. They spoke divers Christian words and seem to understand much more than we, for want of language to comprehend...."*

In 1874 $15,000 was appropriated to build a light station at the "Nubble" and in 1879 construction began. It stands 41 feet tall with the light 88 feet above sea level. Its light can be seen for 13 nautical miles; its flashes Isophase Red 6 seconds 24, 7; its horn sounds every 10 seconds. The walkway railings around the lantern room are decorated with 4-inch brass replicas of the lighthouse itself.

Nubble Light in Space

Nubble Light is a famous American icon and a classic example of a lighthouse. In 1977 the spacecraft, which carried photographs of

Voyager II

Earth's most prominent man made structures and natural features should it fall into the hands of intelligent extraterrestrials,

chose to includes a photo of Nubble Light along with images of other famous icons: the Great Wall of China and the Tai Mahal.

Theodore Parker Burbank

Station Stats

Station Established: 1879

First Lit: 1879

Automated 1987

Foundation Materials: Concrete

Construction Materials: Cast Iron Plate w/ Brick Lining Tower Shape: Cylindrical

Markings/Pattern: White w/ Black Lantern

Original Lens: Fourth Order, Fresnel 1879

Boon Island Light

Ghosts, Shipwrecks and Cannibalism

Boon Island Light is located on a 300-by-700-foot stone outcropping 6.2 miles off the coast of York, in southern Maine. It is the tallest lighthouse in both Maine and New England at 133 feet.. It is said to be one of the most isolated stations off the Maine coast, and also one of the most dangerous and haunted.

Shipwrecks, Cannibalism and Haunting

One source of the Lighthouse's haunting is believed to be the restless spirits of the mariners lost here in 1710. Boon Island Light is most known for the shipwreck the British merchant ship, Nottingham Galley on December 11, 1710. All fourteen crewmen aboard survived the initial wreck, however two died from their injuries and another two drowned attempting to reach the mainland on an improvised raft.

The remaining ten crewmen managed to stay alive despite the brutal winter conditions with no food and no firewood for twenty-four days, until finally rescued by local fishermen.

They resorted to cannibalism, which gave the incident a notoriety that it retains even today. It is said that after this disaster, local fishermen began leaving barrels of provisions on Boon Island in case of future wrecks. Kenneth Roberts fictionalized the harrowing story in his 1956 novel "Boon Island".

In a piece for SeacoastNH.com, writer J. Dennis Robinson relayed accounts from the time of rescuers who described "the ghastly figure of so many objects, with long beards, nothing but skin and bone, wild staring eyes, and countenances fierce, barbarous, unwashed, and infected with human gore."

Three weeks earlier, the 14 mariners were stranded on Boon Island after their merchant ship, the Nottingham Galley, wrecked there. By the time help arrived, there were only 10.

To stay alive, the crewmembers ate their shipmate; a carpenter who'd earlier succumbed to starvation and the elements.

The survivors thru a shipmate into the surf after he died, in hopes that his body would drift ashore and alert locals to the marooned mariners' plight, while two others attempted to fashion a raft from the scattered remnants of the ship and reach land.

The first body never reached shore, Robinson wrote, and the two raft-makers didn't survive their trip for help — but at least one did drift near land in death, motivating locals to form the aforementioned search party.

In the three centuries after the Nottingham Galley crashed, splintering on the rocks and cruelly sinking nearly all of a cargo of potentially life-sustaining butters and cheeses, ship captain John Dean's report of the incident was largely taken as historical fact

The Ghost of the Woman in White

The ethereal young woman shrouded in white who is seen on the rocks at dusk may be Katherine Bright, who came to the 400 square yards of rock as a newlywed with her light keeper husband. A few months later, a wave from a winter storm swept the island, her husband slipped on the rocks and drowned while trying to secure the island's boat.

Katherine somehow managed to pull his body ashore and dragged it to the lighthouse. She left his body at the foot of the stairs, and took over lighthouse duties for five days and nights, without eating or sleeping. On the sixth day, the light went out. Fishermen from York investigated, as the storm was over now, and found Mrs. Bright sitting on the stairs holding the frozen corpse of her husband. She and her husband's corpse were taken ashore, but by that time she'd completely lost her mind. She

died only a few weeks after being rescued. Her screeches can still be heard and her apparition seen at the Light.

History

In 1799 the first day marker and the station itself were established on the island. In 1811 the station was converted to a full light station and a granite tower was constructed.

Both the first tower, and its subsequent replacement, were washed away in storms. The current cylindrical brown granite tower was constructed in 1855.

The Perfect Storm Signals the End

Boon Island Light suffered extensive damage in a blizzard in 1978. Several stones that make up the tower itself were washed into the sea, as were all of the keeper's dwellings and other outbuildings that had been on the island.

There were two Coast Guard keepers on the island when the storm hit, tossing boulders across the island. The men sought refuge in the tower as the angry seas damaged the fuel tanks, helicopter pad and generator building, and destroyed the boathouse and boat launch.

The station was automated in 1980 with the installation of a solar powered beacon and the damaged dwelling was destroyed

Theodore Parker Burbank

Lighthouse Sold at Auction

An online auction for the lighthouse was opened on May 14, 2014. Thirteen bidders participated in the auction, which closed on August 17 with a high bid of $78,000 from a real estate developer from Portland, Maine.

Boon Island Light is not open to the public. The only way to view the tower is by boat or aircraft.

Station Stats

Station Established: 1811
First Lit: 1855
Automated: 1980
Foundation Materials: Surface Rock
Construction Materials: Granite
Tower Shape: Cylindrical
Markings/Pattern: Natural
Original Lens: Second Order Fresnel
The light's beacon flashes white every 5 seconds

Ghost Ship of Harpswell

The Ship of Death – *Those who see it soon perish*

Photo of ship said to be the *Harpswell Ghost Ship* by Cooks Lobster House

During the war of 1812, the privateer vessel *Dash* was famous for sinking British shipping in unequalled numbers. She was often referred to as a "LuckyShip" as she was never damaged nor was a single crewman injured during the capture of the fifteen prizes she took after being commissioned as a privateer by president Madison on September 12, 1814. None of the many shots fired at her ever hit their target; the ship was unscathed.

In January of 1815, not a full four months since being commissioned, the Dash left the shelter of Portland Harbor accompanied by the new privateer schooner *Champlain* for a sort of "Sea Trials." The objective of the sailing was to determine which was the faster ship. On the second day a heavy winter gale buffeted the two ships. *Champlain* altered course and headed for the safety of a port; the *Dash* continued into the teeth of the storm.

No trace of the ship or crew was ever found. The *Dash* was never seen again – or was she? Some believe the *Dash* eventually went down with all hands just off of Bailey Island in Casco Bay while others suggest the vessel was lost on the treacherous shoals of Georges Bank.

Ghost Ship Spotted

However, over the decades usually in the late afternoon and in the evening, an old sailing vessel has been spotted off of Lookout Point in Harpswell Center and Potts Point in South Harpswell, Bailey Island, and Orr's Island. Observers report the ship is unmanned, as no crew has been spotted on board. Also, when approaching the

ship to get a closer look; she will suddenly disappear into thin air.

Many fear the sight of this ghost ship as legend has it as an omen of death for the person, or a member of their family, observing it will die shortly after.

The ship is reported as always being under full sail and sailing straight ahead no matter what the direction of wind or tide. The type of ship sighted will vary. Sometimes it is reported as a four-mast ship, sometimes a two-mast ship or sometimes a brig. It is said that the ship would approach land *"only to vanish in a cloud of fog when coming near the shore or sail backwards into a mist."*

The Death Ship – a poem by

John Greenleaf Whittier (1807–1892)

WHAT flecks the outer gray beyond
  The sundown's golden trail?
The white flash of a sea-bird's wing,
  Or gleam of slanting sail?
Let young eyes watch from Neck and Point,
  And sea-worn elders pray,—
The ghost of what was once a ship
  Is sailing up the bay!

From gray sea-fog, from icy drift,
  From peril and from pain,
The home-bound fisher greets thy lights,
  O hundred-harbored Maine!
But many a keel shall seaward turn,
  And many a sail outstand,
When, tall and white, the Dead Ship looms
  Against the dusk of land.

For never comes the ship to port,
  Howe'er the breeze may be;
Just when she nears the waiting shore
  She drifts again to sea.
No tack of sail, nor turn of helm,
  Nor sheer of veering side;
Stern-fore she drives to sea and night,
  Against the wind and tide.

In vain o'er Harpswell Neck the star
  Of evening guides her in;
In vain for her the lamps are lit
  Within thy tower, Seguin!
In vain the harbor-boat shall hail,
  In vain the pilot call;
No hand shall reef her spectral sail,
  Or let her anchor fall.

Shake, brown old wives, with dreary joy,
  Your gray-head hints of ill;
And, over sick-beds whispering low,
  Your prophecies fulfil.
Some home amid yon birchen trees
  Shall drape its door with woe;
And slowly where the Dead Ship sails,
  The burial boat shall row!

She rounds the headland's bristling pines;
  She threads the isle-set bay;
No spur of breeze can speed her on,
  Nor ebb of tide delay.
Old men still walk the Isle of Orr
  Who tell her date and name,
Old shipwrights sit in Freeport yards
  Who hewed her oaken frame.

What weary doom of baffled quest,
  Thou sad sea-ghost, is thine?
What makes thee in the haunts of home
  A wonder and a sign?
No foot is on thy silent deck,
  Upon thy helm no hand;
No ripple hath the soundless wind
  That smites thee from the land!

From Wolf Neck and from Flying Point,
  From island and from main,
From sheltered cove and tided creek,
  Shall glide the funeral train.
The dead-boat with the bearers four,
  The mourners at her stern,—
And one shall go the silent way
  Who shall no more return!

And men shall sigh, and women weep,
  Whose dear ones pale and pine,
And sadly over sunset seas
  Await the ghostly sign.
They know not that its sails are filled
  By pity's tender breath,
Nor see the Angel at the helm
  Who steers the Ship of Death!

Bell Ringing Lighthouses Dog

Wood Island Light

Five Murders and a Suicide on the Island

A Keeper's Bravery and the Bell Ringing Dog

On March 16, 1865, Lighthouse keeper Eben Emerson saved the crew of the British brig *Edyth Anne* from drowning in a heavy storm off his lighthouse. The Canadian Government later commended him for his gallant bravery and gifted him with a pair of binoculars.

Thomas Henry Orcutt, keeper of Wood Island Light for 19 years had a dog named "Sailor." Sailor became famous for ringing the station's fog bell in an unusual and unique manner. He would greet passing ships by taking the bell cord in mouth and pulling it with his teeth to ring the bell.

Murder – Suicide
Article in the Boston Globe October 23rd, 2005
Written by Douglas Belkin

The day his landlord came looking for the rent, Howard Hobbs was drunk.

It was 1896 and Hobbs had been living on a sliver of an island off the coast of Biddeford, Maine, hunting seals for the $1-a-nose bounty the state was then paying. With his work finally done, the 24-year-old had just spent a couple of days with a buddy on a congratulatory bender on the mainland and had rowed his skiff back to Wood Island. When he bumped into Frederick Milliken it

Theodore Parker Burbank

was nearly dusk.

The rent was overdue, Milliken said. Pay up.

Hobbs, still drunk, took exception — and then, in a fit of pique, he took aim. He shot the 35-year-old landlord and lobsterman once in the abdomen, according to newspaper reports from that week.

Horrified at what he'd done, Hobbs helped carry the mortally wounded Milliken inside, then ran back to his rented shack, placed the same rifle to his mouth and pulled the trigger. The bullet passed through his head and lodged in the ceiling.

The police called it a murder-suicide. The papers called it a tragedy. But the folks around Biddeford called it just the beginning. If you're quiet enough, they will tell you, and stand very still, you will hear the ghosts of Hobbs and  *Milliken: Strange voices carried in the wind. Footsteps echoing where there are no feet. Apparitions, quite literally, that go bump in the night.*

'There are spirits here," said Teresa Lowell, the wife of a lighthouse keeper. She lived on the island from 1984 to 1986 with her husband and believes she bumped into a ghost in her bedroom closet. "I know," she said, "because I felt him."

Several visitors have reported hearing a male voice sobbing, "I didn't mean to do it." Could this be the spirit of Hobbs?

Spanish Ghosts from 1762

The New England Ghost Project from Dracut Massachusetts visited the island and experienced an interesting encounter; - *Suddenly Maureen was not Maureen. Her voice sounded more like a man than a woman and she had taken on a Spanish accent. The spirit she was channeling said he had been on this island 360 days. While it is up for interpretation we assume he meant he was there that many days before he died.*

He said his name was Roger and that the year was 1762. He was very angry because his captain had deserted him and his shipmates on the island. He explained that there were 10 of them to begin with, and he was one of three left. Kolek asked him what flag he flew under.

"I fly under no flag," said the spirit.

"If you fly under no flag, that must mean you're a pirate," said Kolek.

"Choose your words carefully, sir!" warned the spirit.

Then the spirit began to repeat over and over again how cold it was. As he said this, Maureen's hand began to get colder and colder and her grip got tighter and tighter. I started to wonder if it was safe for her body temperature to be so low.

Ron decided this sprit needed to go. He told him to leave her at once.

"No!" the spirit screamed. Maureen's body began writhing, and the noises coming out of her mouth made The Exorcist sound like a Disney movie. When finally Maureen was free of Roger, her hand relaxed and her body temperature returned to normal. A bluish, acrid smoke wisped through the air.

Murdered by an Indian

New England Ghost Project personnel recount another ghostly spirit. This time it was a woman.

It didn't take long before a female spirit approached Maureen. Using the dowsing method to ask the spirit questions, Maureen deduced that the spirit was murdered on the island, that she was lost, and that an Indian killed her.

"It almost feels like she wants our help," she said.

It would appear that this apparition still trying to find her way off the island centuries after being murdered there.

Three More Murders

The NGP team experienced yet another encounter.

Theodore Parker Burbank

Maureen explained that she kept feeling like she was being pulled toward the north end of the island. However, the boardwalk being sometimes 10 feet off the ground, she was often frustrated that she was unable to go where she wanted to. Finally, however, we reached a location where we could step off the boardwalk. Maureen immediately found her spot. Using the dowsing method once again, an eerie location was discovered.

A spirit informed Maureen that more than three girls were buried in this location, and that a shack used to be here. The spirit told Maureen that they were killed separately, and that the shack was set on fire afterwards. "The people that died here were stuck on the island and held against their wishes," said Maureen. "They say they want their story to be told."

History

Wood Island Light, known locally as Stage Island, was built in 1808 under the orders of President Thomas Jefferson. It is located on the eastern edge of 35-acre Wood Island in Saco Bay just outside the entrance to Biddeford Pool and the mouth of the Saco River. Wood Island is an uninhabited island sitting less than a mile off the coast of Biddeford, Maine.

The original tower was an octagonal wooden structure. In 1839 a granite tower was erected replacing the deteriorating wood structure. The 1839 tower was renovated in 1858 to allow for the installation of a 4th order Fresnel lens and the keeper's dwellings were added.

In 1960s the original lantern room was removed and an aero-beacon was installed instead. In 1986 a new lantern room was fabricated and installed on the lighthouse along with the latest technology, a VRB-25 beacon. The United States Coast Guard maintains the lighthouse beacon, while The Friends of Wood Island Light, a non-profit organization, has assisted the Coast Guard by maintaining and restoring parts of the lighthouse and keepers dwellings, which they now own.

Station Stats

Station Established: 1808 - First Lit: 1858 - Automated: 1986
Foundation Materials: Natural/Emplaced
Construction Materials: Granite Rubble
Tower Shape: Conical - Markings/Pattern: White w/Black Lantern

Ram Island Lighthouse

Ghosts and Shipwrecks

This modest lighthouse marks the entrance to both Boothbay Harbor and the Damariscotta River. There are twenty other islands in Maine bearing the name Ram Island and there is a stone tower lighthouse in Casco Bay named "Ram Island *Ledge* Lighthouse."

Before the light was built way back in the 1700's local when fishermen are recorded as anchoring a dory near the dangerous rocks and the first fisherman coming in as darkness fell, would light the lantern to warn others of the rocks. In 1883 congress appropriated $5,000 to build a lighthouse marking the south side of "Fisherman's Passage' and the entrance to Boothbay Harbor.

The Lady in White
Ram Island Light is home to the ghost of a woman dressed all in white. Mariners have reported seeing her waving a fiery torch above her head to warn of the danger, since the 1800's.

In recent years mariners have reported:
A fisherman: *"There was a flash of lightning, and there, standing on the reef at Ram Island, waving her hands in warning was this lady all in white, as if full of electricity. If it weren't for her I would have struck the ledge."*
Second fisherman: *"I was in danger of running into the rocks when I saw a burning boat near shore, about to smash on the rocks and in the boat was this woman, warning me away. I quickly changed direction.*

The next day I saw no trace of the burning boat or the mysterious woman."
Boat owner: *"Seeing her, I spun my wheel just in time to avoid being dashed on the rocks."*
A sailor was approaching Ram one dark, moonless night, when he . . . *saw a woman in white waving a lighted torch over her head.* The sailor veered off just in time to avoid being dashed on the rocks.

Strange, Unexplained Occurrences
Robert Thayer Sterling, author of "Lighthouses of the Maine Coast and the Men Who Keep Them", recounts several ghostly stories of Ram Island:
One captain swore he was warned by a fog whistle at Ram Island during a snowstorm, which was impossible since there was no such signal there.

A four-masted schooner, built at Waldoboro, was on her maiden voyage one quiet starlit summer night . . . *a bolt of lightning illuminated the area moments before our vessel would have struck the ledges.*

Shipwrecks Source of Ghosts?
A year did not go by without at least one major shipwreck being recorded at or near Ram Island. Could some of the island's ghosts be those of unfortunate souls lost in these wrecks?

Some examples:
December 1884 that the schooner *Mineola* was a "totle rack" when it went ashore at Squirrel Island, about a mile to the west.

The schooner *Garland* was wrecked at the nearby rocks known as the Hypocrites in 1885.

In late January 1903, during a heavy gale, the schooner *Harriet W. Babson* ran ashore at Ram Island, smashing through the walkway that connected the tower to the island.

In 1983, the Grand Banks Schooner Museum Trust, associated with the Boothbay Railway Museum, leased the station except for the tower. Under the Maine Lights Program, the property was transferred to the "Grand Banks Schooner Museum Trust" in 1998.

The Museum is a non-profit organization dedicated to the preservation of the maritime history of Maine and New England with close ties to the Canadian Maritimes. The Museum also owns and operates the vessel *Sherman*

The 142-foot schooner *Sherman Zwicker* was built in 1942 at

Zwicker which is pictured here in Halifax Harbor at Tall Ships 2000.

Station Stats
Station Established: 1883
First Lit: 1883
Automated: 1965
Foundation Materials: Granite Block Caisson
Construction Materials: Brick on Granite
Tower Shape: Cylindrical
Markings/Pattern: White w/Natural Caisson & Black Lantern
Original Lens: Fourth Order, Fresnel 1881

Poltergeist

Portland Head Light

Guardian Ghost of "Little Sam"

Portland Head Lighthouse

Many have reported the presence of Portland Head Light house's "Guardian Ghost." The dead son who kept the light burning for more than a week while his father, the Keeper, lay dead at the bottom of the lighthouse stairs.

Portland Head Light was constructed at the Fore River as it exits into Casco Bay in 1791. It is the oldest lighthouse in Maine. It's flashing white light sits 101 feet above high water.

Back in the early nineteenth century it was common for lighthouse keepers to pass their position onto their sons. Such was the case with Jacob Lancaster who was one of the first keepers of Portland Head Light.

Lighthouse beacons back then were actually big oil lamps whose oil had to be replenished constantly. The oil had to be hauled up the one hundred and fifty steps several times a day, plus the wick needed to be trimmed several times a night. The glass had to be

165

cleaned and the brass reflector polished every day. No weekends off. This was a twenty four seven job if there ever was one; lives depended upon the keeper's diligence to his duties.

Jacob passed his job to his son Samuel and he proudly followed in his father's footsteps and carried on the faithful tradition keeping the light burning brightly. His son Sam Junior a/k/a "Little Sam" would help his dad with the duties paying close attention to every detail of the job. His father would constantly boast, "He's a fine boy."

Tragedy struck the Lancaster family; "Little Sam" died of typhoid at the young age of twelve. His widowed father was devastated and could not bear his son being buried far away on the mainland so "Little Sam" was interned feet from the lighthouse.

Later that year during a fierce New England 'Nor Easter Sam senior took ill. He was too weak to climb the flight of stairs and keep the light burning, but try he would and he died trying. Such was the dedication of the Keeper to his duties – the lives of others were at stake.

The storm raged on for several days as 'Nor Easters do yet the now Keeper-less light continued shine brightly. It has been calculated that the light functioned perfectly for the entire week after Sam's death.

Sam had been "feeling poorly" before the storm hit so, after the storm had subsided, a friend decided to visit the lighthouse to see how his friend Sam was feeling. Just as soon as the friend set foot on the island, the light ceased functioning. Apparently the urgent need for "Little Sam's" services were over and he could join his now deceased father on "The Other Side."

Doctors calculated that Sam Senior had been dead for a least a week before he was found. Who maintained the light for that long period? A suggested answer would come from sea captains who had passed by the light during the storm. Several Captains independently reported the same story. They told of a young boy, perhaps no older than twelve, waving reassuringly to them from the "hurricane deck" atop of the lighthouse.

Was this the Spirit of "Little Sam" carrying out the family tradition of keeping the light lit and mariners safe? There are those who believe it was indeed the "Guardian Ghost" of "Little Sam" that kept those passing ships safely on course to safety of the River during that ferocious storm.

Station Stats
Located in Cape Elizabeth Maine

Built in 1791 and is the oldest lighthouse in Maine

Height; 80ft and 101 feet above high water

Light: White rotating every four seconds

The 200,000-candlepower, DCB 224 airport-style aero beacon is visible from 24 miles away.

Of Interest: On a clear day you can see an additional four lighthouses: Ram Island Ledge, Spring Point Ledge, Cape Elizabeth, and Halfway Rock. There's a museum in the keeper's quarters

Operations
Hours of Operation: Lighthouse open on September 14 and museum open daily until October 31 and weekends in November and through mid-December; adults $2.00, children 6-18 $1.00

The Museum at Portland Head Light is open daily from Memorial Day to October 31. Open weekends only from mid-April through Memorial Day and November through mid-December.

Hours are 10 a.m. to 4 p.m.
Admission fee is $2.00 for adults and $1.00 for children age 6-18. Children younger than 6 are free.
The Gift Shop is open when the Museum is open.

For further information call Museum Director Jeanne Gross at 207-799-2661. www.portlandheadlight.com

Theodore Parker Burbank

An Angelic Spirit?

Fort Williams Park

Portland Head Light is located inside this park

Ruins of Goddard Mansion

Construction of the Park began in 1787 at the directive of George Washington, and was completed on January 10, 1791. The grounds and the keeper's house are owned by the town of Cape Elizabeth, while the beacon and fog signal are owned and maintained by the U.S. Coast Guard as a current aid to navigation. It was added to the National Register of Historic Places as Portland Head light on April 24, 1973.

Fort Williams Park covers 90-acres in Cape Elizabeth, Maine, and encompasses several historical sites:

Portland Head Light
Portland Head Light is perhaps the most famous edifice on its grounds, the park also encompasses the decommissioned and largely demolished United States Army post Fort Williams, which was operational during World War I and World War II.

Goddard Mansion
Goddard Mansion, a prominent ruin inside Fort Williams Park, was built in 1853-59 for Colonel John Goddard. Colonel

Goddard was a businessman who commanded the 1st Maine Cavalry Regiment during the American Civil War. Judge Joseph W. Symond purchased the mansion in 1898. The federal government acquired it during the expansion of Fort Williams in 1900. The mansion was converted to quarters for non-commissioned officers and the basement was used as a non-commissioned officer's club. The mansion's remaining walls still stand on the hill overlooking Fort Williams.

Fort Williams

On April 13, 1899, President McKinley re-named the sub post of Fort Preble, Cape Elizabeth's first military fortification, Fort Williams. Named after Brevet Major General Seth Williams, Fort

Fort Williams today

Williams grew to be a tremendous military asset during World War II. Besides protecting the shoreline of Cape Elizabeth, the infantry and artillery units provided the Harbor Defense for Portland. After the war, many of the forts in Casco Bay were closed, including Fort Williams, which traded in its defense of the coast for caretaker status and Army Reserve accommodations. Fort Williams was officially closed and deactivated on June 30, 1963.

New England's Haunted Lighthouses and more

The park has numerous picnic sites with cooking grills. A covered picnic area is also available by reservation from May to October. The covered structure can comfortably seat up to 150 people and is equipped with a cooking grill and picnic tables.

Fort Williams Park is open year round from sunrise to sunset. There is no admission fee.

To reserve the picnic shelter or other areas of the park for group gatherings, please call the Faculties and Transportation Department, 207-799-9574.

Theodore Parker Burbank

Lighthouse in a Fog

Maine's

Mid Coast

Happy Ghost

Hendrick's Head Lighthouse

Ghost of the Lady in White and
The Baby That Washed Ashore

Hendrick's Head Lighthouse was erected on the western side of Southport Island in 1829 at the mouth of the Sheepscot River, the entrance to the shipbuilding center at Wiscasset Harbor. The original lighthouse was built at a cost of $2,662 and first lit on December 1, 1829.

The Baby That Washed Ashore
During a blinding snowstorm in March of 1871, a schooner ran aground on a rocky ledge east of the lighthouse. The turbulent waters crashing on the shore made launching a dory impossible, forcing the keeper and his wife to watch helplessly as the frantic crew scurried about the ship's deck and clamoring up the rigging of the doomed vessel. They watched in horror, as the ship was soon broken to pieces by the relentless pounding of the towering waves.

The keeper built a bonfire on the shore and diligently scanned the waters for signs of life. As darkness fell, the keeper noticed an object being buffeted by the waves being driven towards his position. He braved the icy waters and slippery seaweed covered rocks to wade out and retrieve what was a pair of feather mattresses protectively lashed around a box. He cut off the ropes and discovered a terrified, screaming baby girl inside the box along with a note committing the infant into God's hands. Legend has the baby girl being adopted by a doctor and his wife who were summer residents of the area. They named her Seaborn.

The Ghost of the Woman in White

An apparition of a beautiful young woman dressed in white is often seen walking the shores of the beach near Hendrick's Head Lighthouse. Some think she is the ghost of a woman who was found drowned on that beach. Or, as many believe, she is the ghost of the mother still searching for her shipwrecked baby, the baby that washed ashore 1871.

Medal Winning Dog

On a blustery evening in 1932, Shep, the keeper's family dog became agitated and nervously began a persistent barking, insisting he be let outside. Once outside he raced towards the shore to continue his frantic barking. The keeper was sure the dog sensed something was wrong offshore so he returned to his lighthouse and rang the fog bell as an alarm.

Two powerboats in the area, hearing the bell, scanned the waters to find out what was amiss. They soon found a couple in a skiff being blown out to sea by the strong southwest winds of the day. They had somehow lost their oars and were helpless to prevent being blown far out to sea into the darkening night. The dog's role in the rescue made the news and later the Anti-Vivisection Society of New York awarded Shep a bronze medal.

After being discontinued, the lighthouse and surrounding land was sold to a Dr. William P. Browne of Connecticut in 1935. When electricity reached the area in 1951, Dr. Browne allowed the Coast Guard to automate and re-commissioned the light. A ferocious winter storm in January of 1978 destroyed the boathouse along with the walkway that linked the dwelling to the fog-bell tower. In 1979, the tower's fifth-order Fresnel lens was removed in favor of a modern optic.

Accessibility: The lighthouse and grounds are not open to the public. A view is possible from a beach in West Southport, and some cruises leave from Bath and Boothbay Harbors.

Lighthouse Stats

Station established: 1829
Present lighthouse built: 1875
Discontinued: 1933
Relit: 1951
Construction material: Brick
Height of tower: 39 feet
Height of focal plane: 43 feet
Original optic: Fifth order Fresnel lens (1875)
Present optic: 250 mm
Characteristic: Fixed white with a red sector

Theodore Parker Burbank

Dancing Apparitions?

Marshall Point Light

Rumrunners, Two Ghost and more

Marshal Point Lighthouse is one of twenty-two lighthouses dotting the shores of Penobscot Bay and the one featured in the movie "Forrest Gump" in which the title's character, played by Tom Hanks, determines he has reached the eastern most point of his run, turns around and begins his run back west. "Run Forrest Run."

"Ben," the Ghost of Marshall Point
It was on such a night that a young boy named Ben interrupted a band of Rum Runners off loading their contraband on the shore near the lighthouse. Apparently Ben recognized the bootleggers and they feared he would lead to their imprisonments and so they killed him. Local legend says Ben still roams the narrow road leading to the lighthouse, especially during the darkness of moonless nights.

The Motherly Ghost
The present gift shop building previously served as the lighthouse keeper's residence. Many who have lived here have reported a kind ghostly lady would tuck them in at night.

Theodore Parker Burbank

Was she one of the keeper's wives who continue to reside at the light, or was she one of the many victims of shipwrecks that have occurred off Marshall Point's rocky shore. Would being tucked into bed at night by a motherly ghost help you get to sleep?

History

It is one of the most photographed sites on the New England coast and also the home of Bob Ensor author of two books about the lighthouse dogs Nellie and Molly i.e. "Good Golly Miss Molly" and "Nellie the Lighthouse Dog."

"Rum Runner" by Andrew Wyeth

The lighthouse sits on five acres in Port Clyde and was built in 1857 of granite blocks and brick. It was first lit in 1858 and the light automated in 1980. The light is a 5th order Fresnel Lens whose fixed white light is sits thirty feet above low tide and is visible for fifteen miles. Its fog signal was originally a bell, which was replaced in 1969 by a horn that sounds every ten seconds.

Marshall Point juts far out into Penobscot Bay making it a choice location to establish a prosperous fishing and fish cannery industry. It was also a prime spot for "rum runners" to secret Canadian liquor ashore in the 20's during Prohibition era. Lobster smacks anchored just off shore were often used to hide the liquor to later be rowed ashore, usually on moonless nights.

Station Stats
Station Established: 1832 - First Lit: 1857 - Automated 1980
Foundation: Granite Blocks - Construction: Granite w Brick Tower
Shape: Cylindrical - Markings/Pattern: White w Black Lantern -
Original Lens: Fifth Order Fresnel

Matinicus Rock Lighthouse

A Heroine and an Angry, Locked Up Ghost

Barren, Desolate, Blasted by Harsh Winds

Matinicus Rock Lighthouse sits out in Penobscot Bay, 25 miles offshore of Rockland and about 6 miles from Matinicus, on windswept 33 acre Matinicus Rock Island. In 1614 Capt. John Smith wrote in his log of the "three isles and the rock of Mattinack."

Gale winds, especially in winter, lash the island with such force as to move ten-ton boulders; flood the keeper's house (forty feet above sea level) crash waves over the top of the 48-foot tall lighthouse. In 1874 author Gustav Kobbe wrote, "Life at Matinicus Rock Light is, as it has been for many years, a constant struggle of human nature against the elements which seek to wear it out." It has been called one of the most dangerous spots on the Atlantic Coast.

The island and is best known for being the home of Abbie Burgess, a true heroine and whose story is told in the popular children's book, "Keep the Lights Shining, Abbie".

17-Year-Old Heroine

Abbie Burgess, daughter of Keeper Samuel Burgess, would twice over become a heroine known far and wide. Abbie lived on the island with her invalid mother, father and three younger sisters. In

Theodore Parker Burbank

January 1856, while her father Samuel was away at Rockland acquiring supplies, a terrific storm arose. As the storm grew in intensity, Abbie had the presence of mind to move her siblings and ailing mother out of the keeper's dwelling and into the lighthouse. She also waded knee-deep in the water to rescue her chickens from their coop. Just in time as the storm soon totally demolished the house sweeping it and everything else into the boiling sea. Abbie kept the light burning and took care of keeping her family alive for a month before her father was able to return to the devastated island.

Abbie described the ordeal in a letter to a friend:

The new dwelling was flooded.... As the tide came, the sea rose higher and higher, till the only endurable places were the light-towers. If they stood, we were saved; otherwise our fate was only too certain...During this time we were without assistance of any male member of our family. Though at times greatly exhausted by my labors, not once did the lights fail. Under God I was able to perform all my accustomed duties as well as my father's.

You know the hens were our only companions. Becoming convinced, as the gale increased, that unless they were brought into the house they would be lost.... seizing a basket, I ran out a few yards after the rollers had passed and the sea fell off a little, with the water knee deep, to the coop, and rescued all but one. It was the work of a moment, and I was back in the house with the door fastened, but none too quick, for at that instant my little sister, standing at the window, exclaimed, 'Oh, look there! The worst sea is coming!' That wave destroyed the old dwelling and swept the Rock.

In August of 1856 it Happened Again

With the family running extremely low on food and other supplies, Keeper Burgess and his son and newly appointed Assistant Keeper Benjamin, sailed off in their skiff for Rockland and the needed supplies. Soon after they left the clouds blackened, the wind shifted gale force from the Northeast with heavy rain. The storm raged for three days. Abbie and her family didn't know if the men had made Rockland safely or whether the storm caught them capsizing their small skiff. For twenty one days, subsisting

Abbie Burgess

only on one cup of corn meal and the egg their hens might lay they worried; were the men dead or alive?

Through it all Abbie kept the light lit and her family fed. On the afternoon of the 21st day the little skiff and the men along with the supplies reached the rocky island.

Congress quickly appropriated $35,500 for building a new Keeper's House plus two towers 180 feet apart equipped with a third-order Fresnel lenses. A fog bell was also added and later, in 1869, a steam fog signal was added also.

On July 1, 1883, the light in the north tower was discontinued, and the south light was changed from fixed white to fixed red. On July 1, 1888, this change was reversed, and the north tower was reactivated. On August 15, 1923 the north light was permanently discontinued, and a revolving third-order lens was installed in the south tower.

One hundred years later, in 1983, coastguardsmen removed the Fresnel lens from the south tower and installed a modern beacon. The third-order lens is now part of the collection at the Maine Lighthouse Museum in Rockland.

Access to the island is limited, but the light can be seen via boat cruise

Theodore Parker Burbank

The Angry Ghost of Matinicus Rock Lighthouse
It's just a rock outcropping, and a very harsh environment for anyone; especially so for one keeper, who perhaps couldn't take the desolation, loneliness and life threatening storms. He climbed up into the north tower, strung a rope around his neck and hung himself. His death was discovered a few days later, after the residents of Matinicus Island noticed the light hadn't been lit in a few days and sent a party over the five miles to find out why.

When they arrived they found him hanging in the north tower. Coast Guardsmen keep the door to this tower locked at all times. They say if they don't, his ghost escapes and causes all kinds of havoc. The Guardsmen swear he still clomps around the tower, breaking dishes, turning over chairs and throwing supplies all about. The men stationed here thought they'd finally had stopped the haunting after they were able to lock and bar the door while the ghost was inside slamming about.

Surely he'd stay put, they reasoned. He did, for a while. But then a crewman had to fetch material from the tower and he opened the door and new problems began tormenting the station. The light did not work, machinery malfunctioned and the foghorn developed laryngitis. Only as long as the door stays locked, with the ghost inside, does the lighthouse remain quiet.

New Life for the "Rock"
Under the Maine Lights Program, the lighthouse became the property of the U.S. Fish and Wildlife Service in 1998. The National Audubon Society researches and protects the island's seabird population. The Rock is home to a nesting colony of puffins, as well as terns and scores of other seabirds.

The island is maintained as a bird sanctuary and access is very limited.

New England's Haunted Lighthouses and more

Nature Preserve

Matinicus Rock supports one of the most diverse seabird breeding colonies on the US Atlantic Coast. Atlantic Puffins, Razorbills, Black Guillemots, Leach's Storm-petrels, Arctic, Common and occasionally Roseate Terns, Laughing Gulls, and Common Eiders nest. Matinicus Rock is also the only known nesting place for Manx Shearwater in the United States. Common Murres are regularly present, though not breeding on the island. The island supports over 350 pairs of nesting puffins, 400 pairs of razorbills, 1,000 pairs of terns and about 700 pairs of Laughing Gulls. Black Guillemots and Leach's Storm-petrels are also common. Spring migration can be outstanding; 194 species (including breeding birds) have been recorded on the island since 2000, including notable records for Yellow-nosed Albatross, Red-billed Tropicbird, and Plumbeous Vireo.

Puffin

Station Stats

Established: 1827 - Present lights built: 1857
North light discontinued: 1924 - South light automated: 1983
Construction material: Granite
Height of south light: 48 feet - Height of focal plane: 90 ft
Earlier optic: Third-order Fresnel lens (1857)
Present optic: VRB-25
Characteristic: Flashing white every 10 seconds
Fog signal: One blast every 15 sec

Theodore Parker Burbank

Ghost on Lighthouse Tower?

Fort William Henry

Haunted by the ghost of an Indian Chief

Fort William Henry – 4th Fort to be built on this site

Pemaquid was the most northern coastal settlement of New England during the seventeenth century and the Castine region was the most southern colony of New France (Acadia). At its peak in 1712 (before the Treaty of Utrecht), the territory of *New France*, also sometimes known as the *French North American Empire* or *Royal New France*, extended from Newfoundland to the Rocky Mountains and from Hudson Bay to the Gulf of Mexico.

Fort William Henry is Haunted

Fort William Henry is haunted by the ghost of, Taukolexis, an Indian Chief who English soldiers hung at the fort from a tree in 1696. The chief passed his spirit to the tree right before he was hanged. Some of the visitors, and the employees at the fort, claim to have seen a ghostly figure wandering about the grounds.

Many visitors have reported seeing a wispy figure moving silently through the air, crossing the road over the lawn and then disappear into an ancient tree.

A recent visitor recounts his ghostly experience.

I went with my mom and husband to Fort William Henry. This fort has a tower and what is left of the old foundation of the fort. Next to the tower are what remains of the foundations of the soldier quarters. My mom and husband went into the tower because there was a little museum in there. And, strange for July, there were no other tourists around.

I was fascinated by the soldier quarters and I just stood there staring at the old foundations and wondering and thinking about what it must have been like to be a soldier back then. Suddenly, a man came over from the direction of the tower and stood near the foundations I was looking at. He stood there until I noticed him. I could not see him with my eyes, but he was definitely there and he was a man. When I  *noticed him, he went back over to the tower and stood in the doorway with his arms crossed, just standing there. I had the feeling he belonged in the tower. I was freaked out so I decided to go find my mom and husband, and when I started walking toward the tower... the man disappeared.*

History

During King William's War, the area became a battleground as the French and English fought to determine the boundaries of their empires. In 1689 Baron de St Castin and the Abenaki Indians captured and burned down the wooden stockade fort at Pemaquid. Pemaquid was under French control until 1692 when the English regained control of the region, and began construction of Fort William Henry as a fortress to protect the northern boundary of New England. The Massachusetts government used one third of its budget to build the fort.

Succession of Forts

1633 - The pirate Dixie Bull and his cutthroats destroyed the first European structure built here. Abraham Shurte had built his "Fort" in 1630 as a trading post.

1633 - Fort Pemaguid followed and was destroyed in 1677 during the King Philips War.

1677 - A third fort, Fort Charles, was established with the Treaty of Casco. Fort Charles a wooden stockade, was built by New York governor, Sir Edmund Andros.

It fell to an Indian attack in the spring of 1689. It was lost to the British, in the Siege of Pemaquid, later recaptured it in 1689 during King William's War.

1692 - The British built Fort William Henry during King William's War to defend against the French and Wabanaki Confederacy of Acadia headquartered in what is now Castine. The English built Fort William Henry as a fortress to protect the northern boundary of New England.

Theodore Parker Burbank

Ghostly Lighthouse Cat

Pemaquid Point Lighthouse

The Red Haired Ghost

The Red Haired Ghost

She is often seen in the former keeper's house, now the Fisherman's Museum run by the Town of Bristol. She appears to be a red haired lady who usually appears near the fireplace wearing a shawl. No one is recorded to have died in Pemaquid Light nor the keeper's house and there are no known deaths associated with the Light.

A Shipwreck Casualty?

Perhaps she is a casualty of the shipwrecked *Angel Gabriel*, a British passenger galleon carrying about 100 English settlers and much needed provisions to the New World. The ship went down off the point during a terrible hurricane in August of 1635.

Five persons are said to have perished and all the passengers' belongings lost. Is she waiting for a loved one who was drowned in this calamity? Or maybe someone from the wreck of the *George Edmunds*, which, during a dense fog, crashed on the rocks in 1903.

A frequent visitor to the Museum reports seeing a red haired woman in the main room of the museum. He describes her as having long red hair, heavy build, pale white skin and a sad expression on her face. He says that when he saw her it was in the middle of the day and she was sitting on a chair. She arose, and much to his surprise, walked through the wall and disappeared. He wants to remain anonymous, as he is afraid others will consider him crazy.

History

In 1602 Bartholomew Gosnold, an English Explorer, sailed from Falmouth, England in his Dartmouth bark, the *Concord*, with thirty-two men on board. They intended to establish a colony in New England. At that time Pemaquid was already a port of call for French, Portuguese, Spanish, and English fishermen and the occasional coastal trader. However, it still was surprising to see Native Americans in western garb board the *Concord* and greet him in English. It was Gosnold who named Cape Cod and Martha's Vineyard; Martha was his daughter.

Lighthouse Construction Authorized

May 18, 1826 John Quincy Adams commissioned the construction of the lighthouse and keeper's house and the first Pemaquid's fixed white light went into service on November 29, 1827. The first lighthouse had to be re-built as the contractor had used salt water in mixing the cement and it began to crumbled. Eight years later, in 1835, construction began on a new tower. This time specific instructions prohibited the use of seawater.

The original light could be seen for only 2 miles so, in 1856 it was replaced by a fourth order Fresnel which can be seen for fourteen miles. A new wood frame Keeper's House was added a year later in 1857.

Pemaquid Point is one of New England's most-visited and photographed lighthouses, drawing over 100,000 visitors annually.

Station Statistics
Station established: 1827
Present lighthouse built: 1835
Automated: 1934
Construction material: Stone
Other buildings still standing: 1857 keeper's house, 1896 oil house, fog bell tower (reconstructed 1992)
Height of tower: 38 feet
Height of focal plane: 79 feet
Optic: Fourth-order Fresnel lens (1856)
Characteristic: Flashing white every six seconds

In 2003 Maine residents voted the lighthouse and a three-masted schooner, be featured on the official Maine State coin, the 23rd of 50 state quarters.

Theodore Parker Burbank

Ghost in a Fort's Tunnel

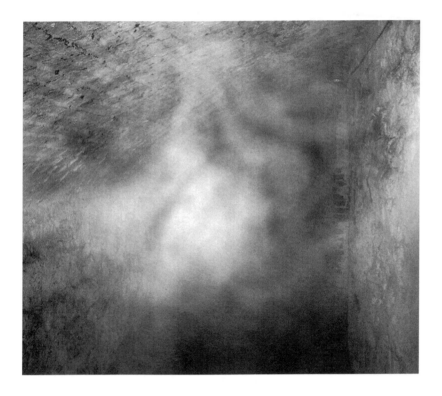

Seguin Island Lighthouse

Ghosts, Sea Serpents and Gold

Haunted Sequin Islands Light in the fog

Piano Playing Ghost

The Legend - A newly married keeper, brought his young wife out
with him to tend the light. Becoming very bored, the wife
complained about not having anything to do. Thinking it would
occupy her, and keep her mind off the boredom, the keeper ordered
a piano to be brought to the island before the next winter set in.
Winching it up the side of the rocky ledge that is Seguin, he proudly
presented it to her.

The wife was delighted, but could not play without sheet music.
Fortunately, one piece of sheet music had come with the piano, so
she set to playing it. By this time, the island was icebound; no other
deliveries could come in. She played her piano, though; the same
song, over and over and over again, driving her husband insane.
Even when he had had new sheet music brought out to the island,
she kept playing the original tune. Finally he'd had enough, took an
axe and chopped the piano to bits.

195

When she complained, he turned to her and chopped her up with the axe, nearly decapitating her. Then he killed himself. It's said, on a quiet night, you can hear the tinkling of the piano floating up the Kennebec River. The keeper has also been seen, still tending to his duties.

From a recent email to a colleague:
"I wanted to mention to you that when I went out to Seguin Island, ME with the USCG a few summers ago, after going to two other lights I did have an uncanny experience at Seguin Light. I should say first that I had heard nothing about any sort of ghosts, nor had I read anything at all about ghosts, and merely went along on this beautiful, sunny day with USCG while they did their repairs to the ATON.

"Just a few days before, a couple had moved in to be at the keepers house at Seguin for the season - they were from California as I recall. I was standing outside the tower at its base and casually speaking with the woman, and, as she was speaking, I heard a piano playing - a rather quick, Scott Joplin style tune - I thought perhaps it might be an unseen radio, although it did have an ethereal quality to it - almost more like a memory on the wind than music. Since she was speaking to me at the time, I did not think to question her about it, or say anything to her. We had just done a walk through the structures, which are impeccably restored.

"When we returned to the USCG office, the Ex-O asked if his staff had told me about the ghost at Seguin which plays the piano!!.... My heart literally stopped when I heard that question...There is no doubt that I had heard it. It is a true story and unforgettable - all the more so in a way, since it was a sunny, almost timeless day, so quiet yet with high winds on the top of that cliff, with the music like a memory more than a song."

More Ghosts on Sequin?
William O Thompson writes in The Lighthouse Digest:
"The keepers I have talked to have also sighted a young girl running up and down the stairs. She has waved to the men on several occasions and some have heard her laughter. It has been reported that a young girl died on the island and her parents buried her near the generator house."

The sites of most reports occurred in the house, light tower, or around the fog sound signal building. The sounds and sightings reported generally indicated ghosts who are comfortably making themselves at home. Sometimes they seemed to be a bit mischievous; moving and replacing tools, taking pea jackets off hooks and dropping them on the floor, or rearranging furniture.

However, it appeared that one or more of the reported ghosts didn't like the idea of the Coast Guard leaving the island in 1985. William Thompson mentions a memorable experience for the warrant officer in charge of the automation.

"All items in the house were being packed for shipment to the mainland. The work crew had retired for the evening and everyone was in bed asleep when the warrant officer was awakened by the shaking of his bed. The apparition in his oil skins was standing at the end of the bed shouting in pathetic tones 'Don't take the furniture, please leave my home alone.' The warrant officer, obviously scared half to death, bolted from his bed and ran to the next room.

It is reported the next day furniture items were loaded in the dory. The engines were started to slowly lower the boat down the skids into the water. Suddenly the engine stopped, the chain holding the dory broke and the loaded boat sped into the ocean and sank with all furniture lost. An almost impossible event taking place in very strange circumstances or something else? Who can be sure?

Lt. Peter Ganzer, Group South Portland Coast Guard Station stated after the men were removed from Seguin, the station's ghost would probably stay to keep an eye on things. In the three years he had been assigned to South Portland Coast Guard Group, he had heard officers tell stories of hearing doors open and close, piano music when there was no piano and someone coughing when all the men were in the same room and none had a cold.

Hunting For Captain Kidd's Gold

This was the title of a Bath Independent article on July 4, 1896. Excerpts follow:

"There still prevails on the coast of Maine a strong belief that there are many treasures, large boxes of gold and silver buried by the notorious pirate Kidd on every island, in every indentation and in every solitary grove.

Dreams have much to do with revealing the long lost treasures and I have seen many a hole that a credulous fisherman had dug, every moment hoping to strike the rusty iron box buried by Capt. Kidd i n the old piratical days."

"Belief in Capt. Kidd's money is fading away. As people learn to reason more accurately, they see that Kidd and other piratical captains sailed the high seas in times when money was scarce, when gold and silver were little mined and comparatively a small amount coined; therefore people would begin to see that it would be impossible that every cove, island and point should be well stored with gold, the booty of pirates upon the high seas."

Seguin Island was long speculated to be the final resting place of both Captain Kidd's and Anne Bonney's booty. Rumors they deposited treasure on Seguin while eluding authorities in the waters of Casco Bay continued well into the 20th century. In 1936, to dispel these rumors, the Bureau of Lighthouses granted Archie Lane an exclusive permit to dig on Seguin for a one year period.

Reports have it that Lane started digging all over the island in a vigorous manner. However, after nine months and no results, Archie Lane abandoned his search. It seems that Lane had not "learned to reason accurately".

Sea Serpent Spotted off Sequin

In July 1875, the American Sentinel reported: *a captain and his one-man crew spotted a sea serpent. The monster came up to their boat and put its head over the rail. The head was the size of a hogshead. On orders of the captain the crewman struck it with his pike and the serpent went back into the water. The*

captain returned to port and showed the spear with the detritus still on it!! He claimed the serpent was 130 feet long!!

Later the American Sentinel carried another article on July 20, 1875: *"The Steamer City of Portland, from St. John to Portland, reports*

198

that when off Seguin Wednesday afternoon she passed the sea-serpent within thirty feet. The monster was lazily floating along on the water when sighted, occasionally lifting its head to look around, and appeared to be making itself at home in that vicinity. Probably he was engaged in a "coast survey."

Battle of the "Boxer" and the "Enterprise"

The following is reported by Mr. & Mrs. Stanwood Gilman in their book "Land of the Kennebec" describing the erroneous battle during the War of 1812.

The American ship "Marguerite", bringing needed goods from Canada, hired the British Captain Blythe of the "H.M.S. Boxer" for one hundred pounds, or about $500, to escort her to the Kennebec and protect her from privateers. Near the mouth of the Kennebec, Capt. Blythe fired a couple of shots to make things look well, and it appeared that all would go off as planned.

But Capt. Burroughs of the "U. S. brig Enterprise" in Portland heard the shots and hurried over, squaring for battle. Here, off Seguin, the famous sea battle between the "Boxer" and the "Enterprise" took place. Both young captains were killed, and the "Enterprise" won the victory.

Longfellow chronicles this battle in a poem:

> *I remember the seafight far away:*
> *How it thundered o'er the tide;*
> *And the dead captains, as they lay*
> *In the graves o'erlooki ng the tranquil bay*
> *Where they in battle died*

NOTE: The captains were buried side-by side in Portland.

Theodore Parker Burbank

History

The earliest visitor is recorded to be George Popham and Ralegh Gilbert who reportedly on August 15, 1607 anchored under Seguin Island before moving into the Kennebec River.

Seguin Light sits on a sixty-four acre island 10 miles from Boothbay Harbor and three miles from the closest shore. In 1795 President George Washington commissioned construction of the light. The first tower was built at a cost of $6,000; it was 165 feet above sea level.

The first lights were oil lamps with no chimneys, sixteen in number, with crude reflectors placed in a circle on a wooden bench. The lantern was a fixed white light with the power of the light sent in the ocean direction, the landside being dark.

1819 a new fifty-three foot stone tower was erected fifty feet from the original structure and a new "modern" First Order Fresnel Lens was installed and remains Maine's only First Order Fresnel lens, and the highest light above sea level in Maine. This extremely rare lens stands 9 feet tall and can be seen for more than twenty nautical miles out to sea. During thick or foggy weather the Fog Signal will be sounded for eight seconds at fifty-two seconds intervals.

Visit the Island by Ferry

The Island opens in May. There are several Charter/Ferry services with knowledgeable guides.

Station Stats

Station Established: 1795 - First Lit: 1857
Automated: 1985
Foundation Materials: Surface Rock
Construction Materials: Granite Black/Brick
Tower Shape: Cylindrical
Markings/Pattern: White w/Black Lantern
Original Lens: First Order, Fresnel 1857

Owl's Head Lighthouse

**Two Ghosts – Couple Brought Back from the Dead –
Spot the Bell Ringing Dog**

Owl's Head Lighthouse is a 30-foot tall cylindrical brick tower on a granite foundation standing on top a cliff. Owls Head Lighthouse is a place of outstanding beauty and its history is filled with remarkable and mysterious events.

The Friendly "Little Lady" Ghost

She is suspected of being the wife of a former keeper and is referred to as "Little Lady," who is usually seen in the kitchen. Doors have slammed shut unexpectedly, silverware gets rattled, but mostly the Little Lady gives a feeling of peace when she has been encountered. She is occasionally seen looking out of the kitchen window. But she's not the only apparition.

The Brass Polishing Ghost

Many later keepers have encountered the spirit of this nameless brass-polishing keeper. They generally report seeing the ghost out of the corner of their eyes. His footprints have been seen outside in the snow. He also is noted for polishing the brass in the light tower. Polishing brass, called bright work, was the bane of light keepers. The Lighthouse Board insisted it be polished daily, so it's very possible this is one very welcome ghost.

Aerial view of Owls Head Light Station - Photograph courtesy U.S. Coast Guard

One time, a 3-year-old girl woke up her parents and told them they needed to get up because it was going to get foggy, and they needed to ring the fog bell. When questioned on how she knew, she explained her sea captain "imaginary friend," had told. Later she pointed at a photograph of an old-time Keeper and exclaimed; *that's him.*

The lighthouse keeper's house is currently used as quarters for the Rockland Coast Guard Chief Warrant Officer, and either this ghost or the ghost of the "Little Lady" keeps lowering the thermostat. Apparently frugality continues into the afterlife.

Historian Bill O. Thomson says: *I've often seen footprints that appear after a rain or snowfall. The prints of large workman's boots lead in only one direction, up the ramp, up the stairs, and to the tower where the brass will be found polished and the lens cleaned. The typical keeper who lived back in these times was a dedicated worker,"* said Thomson. *He loved his lighthouse and didn't want anything to ever go wrong with it. Keepers knew that if anything fouled up the equipment or disturbed the light, a disaster could occur. So they never wanted to leave their post. I think sometimes when they died their spirits stayed behind.*

Couple Brought Back From the Dead

From the Lime Rock Gazette, December 22, 1850 - *"One of the most terrible storms we have ever witnessed hit Rockland. A small schooner set anchor in the harbor early in the storm, and its captain went ashore leaving the mate Richard B. Ingraham, a crewman Roger Elliot, and a passenger Lydia Dyer—Ingraham's fiancée. As the storm intensified, the schooner was torn from its mooring and dashed onto the rocks near Owls Head Light. Its three occupants huddled close together and pulled blankets around them for warmth and protection. As the schooner was breaking up, Elliot sought help by going to shore.*

The keeper, who was out driving his sleigh, spied Elliott and took him to the lighthouse to revive him. Nearly unable to speak, Elliot pled for help to be sent for Dyer and Ingraham. A search party was organized, and the two were discovered encased in a block of ice formed from the spray.

Although the couple appeared dead, the rescuers refused to give up. They chipped off the ice and put the man and woman in cold water. Bit by bit, they increased the temperature and massaged and exercised the pair's limbs. After nearly two hours, Dyer showed signs of life. An hour later, Ingraham opened his eyes and asked, "What is all this? Where are we?" It took months for the couple to regain their health, but Elliot never fully did. Dyer and Ingraham went on to marry and raise four children.

Spot – the Bell Ringing Dog

A Springer Spaniel named Spot belonged to the two daughters of Keeper Augustus Hamor. Daughters Pauline and

Stone Marks Spot's Grave

203

Theodore Parker Burbank

Millie taught Spot to pull on the rope to ring the fog bell whenever a vessel passed or during a fog. The dog took his job quite seriously. When it was foggy Spot would happily pull on the rope for hours at a time.

Spot's favorite visitor was the mail boat. Its skipper Stuart Ames always had a special treat for him and Spot came to recognize the sound of the boat's engine. One stormy Christmas, the mail boat out of Matinicus was late, due to the fog. Spot heard the boat, and ran out to do his self-appointed duty. Unfortunately, the rope and the bell were frozen and he couldn't ring the bell. Spot ran out to the edge of the cliff and started barking loudly. The mail boat's captain heard him, and realized where he was and turned before crashing into the rocks. Spot is buried next to his fog bell.

History

It has one of the last six Fresnel Lenses in operation in Maine. In

1854, a keeper's house was built separate from the lighthouse. The cottage now serves as Coast Guard housing. A fourth order Fresnel lens was installed in 1856. A generator house and an oil storage building were added in 1895.

Owls Head Light was built in 1825, for $2,707.79 on 17.5 acres of pine-covered headland, on the south side of the entrance to Rockland Harbor in Owls Head, Maine. The lighthouse was approved by President John Quincy Adams in 1824 and built in

1825. The US Coast Guard operates it and it is also part of Owls Head Light State Park.

The lighthouse is located in Owls Head Light State Park. There is a large parking area near the lighthouse, and the grounds are open to the public. From spring to fall, the lighthouse is open on selected days; check the Friends of Rockland Harbor Lights site for the schedule.

Station Stats
Station established: 1825
Present lighthouse built: 1852
Automated: 1989 –
Construction material: Brick
Height of tower: 30 feet
Height of focal plane: 100 feet
Optic: Fourth order Fresnel lens
Characteristic: Fixed white
Fog signal: Two blasts every 20 seconds
Visible for 16 miles

Theodore Parker Burbank

Sea Captain's Ghost?

Fort Knox State Park

Built to Prevent British Establishment of
"New Ireland' and, it's HAUNTED

The fort is located on the western bank of the Penobscot River in the town of Prospect overlooking Bucksport, Maine. During the country's infancy, Maine was repeatedly involved in northeast border disputes with British Canada who wanted to establish *New Ireland* on the land north of the Penobscot River.

Fort Knox is Haunted

Loud and mysterious sounds echo through the empty "Long Alley" where strange anomalies appear on thermal imaging cameras and ghosts have repeatedly been sighted.

SyFy Channel's "Ghost Hunter" TV show featured the investigation of Fort Knox. "They definitely believe it's haunted," said Leon Seymour, executive director of the Friends of Fort Knox, who appeared on the program as guide for the "Ghost Hunter" crew as they toured the fort.

While in the "Long Alley" the crew heard some "crazy breathing" and something broke though their laser grid. "It sounds like it's right next to me," said Jason Hawes, one of the shows stars, as he walked down the darkened alley. "It sounds like it's coming closer and closer." Later, near the cannon mounts, the TV crew also heard loud footsteps yet no one was there.

Haunted "Long Alley" inside Ft Knox

Ghost of Custer's Ordnance Sergeant

Liza Walsh, author of "Haunted Fort: The Spooky Side of Maine's Fort Knox," in an interview with the Portland Herald, tells the story of ordnance sergeant Leopold Hegyi, caretaker at the fort from 1887-1900. Hegyi served in the cavalry and helped train Custer's army in Missouri before moving to Maine.

"He was from Hungary, and he was alone for 13 years, mostly, except for the Spanish American war when there were a few people there" at the fort, Walsh said. "His story was very compelling to me. He seemed like such a character and an engaging man. His wife lived in New York. She wouldn't come be with him. And every day, twice a day, he patrolled that fort all by himself. And then he would go and have a beer at the Prospect store."

"Many people think Hegyi is the ghost in the duster coat that's often seen wandering the dark, wet pathways of the stone fortress."

"People get scared, but now that I've read his story and learned about him, I don't think he's someone to be afraid of," Walsh said. "I think he's keeping an eye on the fort like he's always done."

Portland Herald: Why is the fort so haunted?

A: "There is the theory that granite is a conductor for ghosts, and that much granite attracts spirits. Also, there's the "theory" that the confluence of swirling water and massive amounts of granite are conducive to ghosts. There's theories that it's like a vortex, that it's some kind of an energy field that makes this place ripe for haunting. And then I think it's the layout of the fort, all those dark tunnels. It's dark and wet so much of the year, and cold. Apparently spirits are more active in that kind of climate and environment."

Ghost family in the Fort

Portland Herald: Would you say you believe in

A: :Ghosts? Oh yes, I definitely do."

Portland Herald: What was your spookiest experience there? Was it being locked in?

A: "I think so, and then my husband making us go into all the little rooms that I think were store rooms, but they don't have any light and then you step into them. They're almost like a little dungeon. I did hear things.

We did hear footsteps when I was on various ghost hunts. We would hear things upstairs, and everybody heard it. And then (we heard) things through their equipment. They use these radio frequencies – a ghost box, it's called – the radio frequencies apparently allow the energies to talk through. There were things said that you could pretty clearly hear, like a soldier talking about the Civil War, little snippets that just seemed like someone was trying to communicate. It would be hard to kind of create that."

East Coast Ghost Trackers, LLC provides private tours of the fort for groups and on a regular schedule at the fort. They can be contacted by Email: eastcoastghosttrackers@yahoo.com: Phone (207) 974-3074 or, call the fort (207) 469-6553.

History
Built to Prevent the Establishment of *New Ireland*

Many battles were fought to keep the area north of the Penobscot River as a part of America's *New England* and not British *"New Ireland."* The area between Castine and the rich lumber city of Bangor was invaded and occupied by the British during the American

New Ireland as Envisioned by the British

Revolution and the War of 1812. Congress authorized construction of the fort in 1844 to protect the region north of the Penobscot River against possible future British attempts to establish New Ireland.

First Attempt to Establish New Ireland
June 16, 1779 – the British invade Castine to establish *New Ireland.* American Colonialists in Massachusetts hastily assembled *The Penobscot Expedition* of 1779 in order to force the British from Castine, where they had begun building a fortification later named Fort George.

July 25, 1779 – The American fleet arrived in Penobscot Bay.
Major Flaw in the Plan - *No one is in Overall Command*
In the haste to charter the commanders of the expedition, the Massachusetts legislators failed to appoint a Supreme Commander of the overall expedition. This meant that no one was in overall command of the expedition. This major oversight would combine with other factors resulting in the worst American Naval defeat until the Japanese attacked Pearl Harbor in December of 1941.

Fort Knox and the Penobscot Narrows Bridge and the Location of the Penobscot Expedition's defeat

August 14, 1779 - The Expedition fiddled and diddled allowing a British reinforcement fleet to arrive. The conflict took place at the mouth of the Penobscot River with many of the Colonial ships fleeing up river towards Bangor. The Americans lost 43 ships and suffered approximately 500 casualties. The scene of the Battle can be viewed from the observation Tower of the Narrows Bridge adjacent to Fort Knox.

Theodore Parker Burbank

The *Penobscot Expedition* experience was pivotal in the movement to separate Maine from Massachusetts, primarily because it was a military and financial disaster that essentially bankrupted Massachusetts. This meant Massachusetts could no longer protect Maine from the British.

Second Attempt to Establish New Ireland
October 1814 - During the War of 1812, Sir John Sherbrooke led a British force from Halifax, Nova Scotia to re-establish *New Ireland*. The Battle of Hampden occurred in August of 1814, concurrent with the retaking of Castine. A particularly brutal British Captain Robert Barrie, saw to it that after defeating a small local militia and sinking an American Frigate, Mainers would pay for their "crimes". His troops sacked the towns of Bangor and Hampden, burning, smashing and looting.

When local leaders begged him to show a little humanity he said, *"Humanity! I have none for you. My business is to burn, sink, and destroy. Your town is taken by storm. By the rules of war we ought to lay your village in ashes, and put its inhabitants to the sword. But I will spare your lives, though I mean to burn your houses."*

State of Maine Established
The Battle of Hampden was the last straw and the separation from Massachusetts movement was successful. Massachusetts' failure to provide adequate protection against British raids provided the separation movement the momentum and support required to break away from Massachusetts. Maine became the twenty-third state in the Union on March 15, 1820.

Fort Knox, built 1844 - 1869
The Aroostook War of 1838-1839 revived concern over the vulnerability of the region to another attack like that of 1814. Tensions were high between the British and the Americans given the several attempts by the British to claim what is now "Down East" Maine even though yet another Peace Treaty had just been negotiated. Construction funding from Congress was intermittent, and although nearly a million dollars were spent, the fort's design was never fully completed. It is named after Henry Knox, the first US Secretary of War.

Across the River from the fort is a haunted monument.

Jonathan Buck Gravestone Cursed

Monument replaced twice – Curse image reappears

Who was Colonel Jonathan Buck

Born in Woburn, Mass., Feb. 20, 1719, raised in Haverhill, Mass. Oct. 19, 1742, Buck married Lydia Morse. They had nine children, six of whom survived childhood.

In July of 1762, Buck sailed the sloop Sally up the Penobscot River to survey six plantations (now Bucksport, Orland, Castine, Sedgwick, Blue Hill and Surry). In 1764 he established the first settlement on Plantation No. 1 now known as Bucksport.

Woman's leg appears as proof of the curse

In July of 1779 Colonel Buck was part of the disastrous Penobscot Expedition's defeat by the British. He and his Bucksport militia were laying siege to Fort George in Castine. The day after the Patriots defeat at the mouth of the Penobscot River, Buck his wife and seriously ill daughter, Lydia, fled to safety and, even with Jonathan suffering from gout, walked the 200 miles from Bucksport to Haverhill.

He returned to Bucksport (Plantation No. 1) five years later and rebuilt everything that had been destroyed by the British in 1779. In 1792 Plantation No. 1 was renamed Buckstown in Col. Jonathan's

Theodore Parker Burbank

honor. March 18, 1795, at 4:30 p.m., Buck died. He was buried in a cemetery east of Buckstown.

Short Version of the Curse

Jonathan Buck was a Puritan to whom witchcraft was an abomination. Therefore, as one version of the legend goes, he sentenced a woman accused of witchcraft to be executed and the deformed son of the witch called down the curse upon the Colonel. *"Your Tomb shall bear the mark of a witch's foot for all eternity!"*

Haverhill Gazette Version of the Legend

"The hangmen was about to perform his gruesome duty when the woman turned to Col. Buck and raising one hand to heaven, as if to direct her last words on earth, pronounced this astounding prophecy: 'Jonathan Buck, listen to these words, the last my tongue will utter. It is the spirit of the only true and living God which bids me speak them to you. You will soon die. Over your grave they will erect a stone that all may know where your bones are crumbling into dust. But listen, upon that stone the imprint of my feet will appear, and for all time, long after you and you accursed race have perished from the earth, will the people from far and wide know that you murdered a woman. Remember well, Jonathan Buck, remember well."

Oscar Morill Heath's Version of the Legend

A much different and lurid version of the legend is told by Oscar Morill Heath in *Composts of Tradition: A Book of Short Stories Dealing with Traditional Sex and Domestic Situations.* This accounting of the legend is so shocking that those recounting the Buck legend avoid many of the details in this version of the legend.

In one variation Heath alleges the doomed woman had a son fathered by Buck and she was pregnant with another child by him. It is said that Buck, in his position as Justice of the Peace, convicts her, orders her tied to the door of her home and the house set on fire.

Her leg rolls out of the bonfire. The son grabs his mother's burning leg and begins beating Buck with it. Buck is severely injured and is permanently crippled by his injuries. The son keeps the leg, and after Buck dies and is on view in his coffin, the son touches Buck's corpse with the old leg. Miraculously, Buck is said to emerge from his coffin and confess everything. Buck reportedly then return to his coffin and says to the woman's deformed son, "Close the lid, boy."

A. Hyatt Verrill's Version of the Legend

In A. Hyatt Verrill's version, a "half-witted" man is brought before Buck accused of murdering a woman and removing one of her legs. Buck condemns the man, who says that the appearance of the leg on Buck's tombstone will be his vengeance.

Heirs have tried to clean the foot off the stone and have had the monument replaced twice -- but the foot keeps reappearing!

Ghostly Bride?

Maine's

Bold Coast

a/k/a

Down East

Theodore Parker Burbank

Ghost in a Passageway

Mount Desert Rock Lighthouse

Spooky, Desolate Rock

US Coast Guard photo

In 1604 the French explorer Samuel de Champlain named Mount Desert Rock as well as the distant, much larger Mount Desert Island.

Congress appropriated $5,000 for a lighthouse on Mount Desert Rock in 1829, to aid navigation to Frenchman and Blue Hill Bays from the south. Its fixed white light, forty-four feet above high water, went into operation the following year.

Mount Desert Rock is a small 600 yards long by 200 yards wide rocky outcropping located twenty-six miles at sea off of Mt Desert Island. Its highest point is only twenty feet above the sea at low tide. With high tides rising twelve feet on average the entire "island" is often submerged during storms. The station is farther offshore and more exposed to violent weather than any other lighthouse on the

219

east coast. Fishermen would bring the keepers baskets of soil which they would carefully placed into protected crevasses in the rock and plant flowers or vegetables. It was sometimes a loosing battle as a storm could suddenly spring up and wash away both the soil and the plants. Life was hard on the rock.

Tragedy at the Rock
During the Age of Sail in1880s, the schooner *Helen and Mary*, carrying granite from Halifax to Boston, was caught in a violent storm near the "Rock" and sank. The captain, his wife, their baby girl and the wife's brother, the first mate, were on board. The vessel sank throwing them all into the frigid waters of Penobscot Bay. The first mate was able to grasp onto some floating wreckage but saw no signs of his relatives; was he the lone survivor?

Clinging onto the wreckage the mate spotted a package floating by. Instinctively, he lifted it out of the water and, upon unwrapping it, was shocked to discover it contained his sister's baby girl. She was alive! She was wrapped in an oilskin that had kept her dry and the air trapped inside the bundle kept the package that contained her afloat. The mate held the baby out of the water and close to him throughout the long night and into the next day when they were spotted and rescued by the crew of the lighthouse tender *Iris*.

Another Tragedy
In December 1902, the New York tugboat *Astral*, with a barge in tow, ran aground at Mount Desert Rock in a gale with 18 men aboard. All the men except one, who had already frozen to death, were pulled to safety. How many other sailors have perished on or near this desolate rock over the centuries?

Is the Rock Haunted?
Edward Rowe Snow, lighthouse historian and the "Flying Santa" who airdropped Christmas presents to lighthouse keepers and their families for decades remarked, *"I have made several flights over this far-distant isle of the deep, and can never overcome a feeling of uneasiness while circling above the rocky ledge in a small land plane."*

Was the uneasy feeling a reaction to the presence of spirits past? Perhaps drowned ancient mariners or, was it a reaction to the spirit of a young mother still searching for her baby daughter?

Station Stats

1830 – Original lighthouse, lantern on top of keeper's house,
1847 – Granite conical tower built for $10,000.
1858 – New lantern installed on tower and 3rd order Fresnel lens installed. Bell tower built and fog bell installed.
1876 – New Keeper's house built.
1877 – Larger bell and bell tower installed.
1889 – Fog bell replaced by steam whistle.
1891 – Fog signal building built.
1893 – New keeper's house built.
1902 – Tug boat Astral ran aground in the fog. All but one of the crew rescued by keeper and his wife.
1931 – Generators installed to provide electricity.
1962 – Hurricane Daisy blew through and swept two empty 1500-gallon fuel tanks, a paint locker, concrete walkway and the covered walkway between the tower and keeper's house into the sea. c. mid-1970s – Fresnel lens replaced by aero-beacons, lantern removed.
1977 – Light automated

1985 – New lantern put on.

The property has taken a beating in some recent storms, particularly Hurricane Bill in 2009. If you would like to find out more about how you can help the whale research effort at Mount Desert Rock, please call Allied Whale at 207-288-5644.

The lighthouse is best seen by private boat or from the air, although whale watches from Bar Harbor occasionally pass near Mount Desert Rock.

Angelic Ghost

Prospect Harbor Lighthouse

Ghost of Captain Salty

The lighthouse is located on the grounds of a Navy installation. The keeper's house, known as "Gull Cottage," is available for overnight stays for active and retired military families.

The Navy provides a Guest Log wherein guests can record their vacation experiences. According to Gull Cottage Log entries guests there have experienced significant ghostly activity during their stay.

Haunted

Entries in the Guest Log sums up the haunting quite well. *The first time my sister and I heard the ghost was in 1976. We were sleeping in the room with the twin beds. In the middle of the night we heard what sounded like motorcycles coming down the road. In the morning we were switched in our beds.*

In 1980 is when I saw the sea captain ghost on the woodstove that was in the living room. I was sleeping in the den area downstairs on the sleeper sofa with my sisters and two friends.

I had to use the bathroom upstairs where my parents were sleeping. I came down the stairs and saw the captain with his legs crossed and smiling at me! I never ran so fast in my life up the stairs to where my parents were sleeping.

My dad had to practically sit on me to calm me down I was so shook up!!! In the morning we saw where he had sat. The ghost is believed to be that of the former caretaker John Workman's father referred to as "Captain Salty."

On New Year's Day 1951 "Captain Salty," who's real name was Ira Workman, was sitting in his rocking chair in front of the wood stove lighting his pipe when suddenly he suffered a massive heart attack and died.

Many guests have reported smelling tobacco smoke in the front room even though no one is there and none of their party smoked.

Other guests have written about strange events that occur during the night the night, like doors opening and closing, lights going on and off. Three statues that sit on a windowsill at Gull Cottage are constantly found rearranged and in different positions than they were the night before.

Prospect Harbor Light is located near Gouldsboro, on Prospect Harbor Point, a small peninsula that divides Sand Cove from Inner Harbor. It is an active U.S. Coast Guard aid to navigation. Its Light flashes red every 6 seconds with 2 white sectors. The red light has a range of 9 nautical miles. The white light has a range of 7 nautical miles. There is no fog signal.

History

The first lighthouse to mark harbor entrance was built in 1850, deactivated between 1859 and 1870, and reactivated May 15, 1870 "to serve as a guide to the harbor of refuge which it marks."

The original stone tower and residence were in terrible condition and in 1891 construction of a new light and residence were authorized to replace them. The new light was lit July 25, 1891.

The brick oil house was added in 1905. The light was automated in 1934 however, keepers remained on site until 1951, when its Fresnel lens was removed and replaced by modern optics. The station last underwent major restorative work in the early 2000s; it remains an active aid to navigation.

Station Stats:

Established: 1850

Present lighthouse built: 1891

Automated: 1951

Construction material: Wood

Other buildings still standing:

1891 keeper's house, 1905 oil house, boathouse

Height of tower: 38 feet

Height of focal plane: 42 feet

Earlier optic: Fifth-order Fresnel lens (1870)

Present optic: 250mm (below)

Characteristic:

Flashing red every six seconds with two white sectors

Haunted Minot's Light

Winter Harbor Light

Ghostly Partiers Knocking at the Door

Ghosts Knocking but Not Let In

Bunny Richmond, a lighthouse keeper's daughter, kept a log, recording storms and other occurrences, such as visits by ghostly spirits at the light: *"They seemed to be a mixed group of people who came down the walk under my window chatting casually, their feet audibly scraping the cement. They knocked at the back door in a moderate way and talked among themselves as they waited for me to come and open it. My callers weren't discouraged because I wouldn't open the door and repeated the knocks several times before going away. I don't know yet where my unreal callers came from or why they gave up knocking."*

Her brother also heard voices in the lighthouse and is said to not understand how his sister could want to be there alone. Another former lighthouse keeper spoke of "unreal callers" who would knock on the door, but where not visible to the eye. Holden, while lying in bed at night, at times, could hear the voices of ghosts coming from inside the house from kitchen below.

History

Winter Harbor Lighthouse, a/k/a Marks Island Light, is located near the entrance to Frenchman Bay, across from Bar Harbor and was built in 1856 at a cost off $4,500. Its white, cylindrical, brick tower is nineteen-foot-tall, tower, and thirty-seven feet above high water. Its fifth-order Fresnel lens with a fixed white light was deactivated and replaced by a lighted bell buoy in 1933 The property was sold at auction for $552 in 1934 to a Bar Harbor resident.

Owned by Authors and Playwrights

The property has been owned by a series of authors and playwrights. Writer and musician Bernice "Bunny" Richmond author of "Winter Harbor" and "Our Island Lighthouse."

The next owners were Patricia and René Prud'hommeaux. Pat wrote, under the pen name Joan Howard, "The Light in the Tower", a children's book about Christmas on the island René authored "The Sunken Forest" and "The Port of Missing Men."

Security analyst turned writer, playwright and artist William C. Holden, III, acquired the property in 1995. The property had been abandoned for over a decade when Holden acquired it. He spent another decade and about $650,000 to purchase and renovate the property. He installed an orange light in the tower in 1996; orange to denote that it was a private light and not an official U.S. Coast Guard light.

In October 2004, the island was sold to an interior designer from New York City for $1.25 million.

The lighthouse can be seen distantly from the loop road on Acadia National Park's Schoodic Peninsula. It can also be seen from tour boats leaving Bar Harbor.

Station Stats

Station Established: 1856 - First Lit: 1856
Deactivated: 1933
Foundation Materials: Brick
Construction Materials: Brick/Asphalt
Tower Shape: Cylindrical
Markings/Pattern: White w/Black Lantern
Original Lens: Fifth Order, Fresnel 1856

Phantom Ship

West Quoddy Lighthouse

Mysterious Woman in Seaweed

The West Quoddy Light sits at the eastern most point in the United States. The light flashes two seconds on, two seconds off, two seconds on then off for nine seconds. The light sits atop a forty-nine foot tower with distinctive red and white strips and can be seen eighteen miles out to sea.

Ghost Draped in Seaweed
Sometime after the lighthouse was built a woman wearing a formal Victorian dress mysteriously washed up on the shore near the new lighthouse. How she had met her unfortunate fate was a mystery as there had been no storms or reports of shipwrecks for some time in the area. Was she somehow connected with the smuggling activity that was so prevalent with the Canadian Campobello and Deer Islands so close by?

The town's people buried this mystery woman near the lighthouse at the West Quoddy Lifesaving Station believing the burial to be the end of the story; but it wasn't.

Theodore Parker Burbank

Many locals, park rangers and a park manager report having seen her shadowy figure as she walks the trails of the light station. The reports are the same. She moves silently, dressed in a flowing Victorian style dress. The wind billows her dress and seaweed is draped elegantly over her shoulders. She will stop occasionally to peer out to sea. What is she looking for?

History

Congress authorized $5,000 in 1806 for the construction of light Station at West Passamaquoddy Head. It was completed on April 21, 1808. The current tower was built in 1858. Eight red stripes alternate with seven white stripes. The stripes are about 25 inches wide. The bottom stripe and the top stripe are red.

Station Stats

Station Established: 1808 Year
First Lit: 1858
Automated: 1988
Foundation Materials: Masonary
Construction Materials: Brick Tower
Shape: Conical
Markings/Pattern: Red & White Bands w/Black Lantern
Original Lens: Third Order, Third Order, Fresnel 1858
Focal Plane: 83 feet above sea level
Visibility: Approximately 18 miles; 35,000 candlepower
Foghorn: Automated

Answers to the Quiz

LIGHTHOUSE - MA	GHOST
Baker Island Light	A Kissing Ghost
Bird Island Lighthouse	Chain Smoking Keeper's Wife
Minot's Ledge Lighthouse	Ghost the Screams "Keep Away" in Portuguese
Scituate Lighthouse	The Army of Two
Boston Light	Classical Music Loving Ghost
Long Island Light	Woman in Scarlet
Plymouth Lighthouse	First Woman Lighthouse Keeper Still on the Job
Nauset Light	Pirate's Lover became a witch and later swallowed by a whale
Nixes Mate	Sailor's curse shrinks Light's Island into the sea
Nauset Light	Ghost of pirate haunts outer Cape
Eastern Point Light	Ghosts of a mother and daughter and their German Sheppard dogs
Race Point Light	Replaces worn or storm tattered flags
Lighthouse - CT	
New London Ledge Lighthouse	Ghost of Keeper who's wife ran off w ferry captain
Stratford Shoal Light	The "city slicker" second assistant keeper
Penfield Reef Lighthouse	Drowned keeper still on duty
Lighthouse - ME	
Boon Island Light	The woman in White
Cape Neddick Light a/k/a Nubble Light	Three masted bark "Isadore"
Hendrick Head Lighthouse	Baby that washed ashore and the "Woman in White"

Marshall Point Light	Teenage Boy and Rum Running Murderers
Matinicus Rock Lighthouse	Angry Keeper's ghost kept locked in the tower
Mount Desert Rock Lighthouse	Ghost of the mother who's infant girl survived the sinking of the Helen and Mary
Owl's Head Lighthouse	Brass polishing ghost
Pemaquid Point Lighthouse	Red Hair Lady in Shawl Near Fireplace
Portland Head Light	Guardian ghost of "Little Sam"
Prospect Harbor Lighthouse	Two ghosts? Captain Salty and grandfather Ira
Ram Island Lighthouse	Lady in white waving a fiery torch
Sequin Island Lighthouse	Wife Who Has Only One Piece of Sheet Music
West Quoddy Lighthouse	Mysterious woman in seaweed
Winter Harbor Light	Ghostly partiers knocking at the door
Wood Island Light	Ghosts of five murdered and one who committed suicide
Portland Head Light	The Guardian Ghost of "Little Sam"

Lighthouse/Fort - NH

Portsmouth Harbor Lighthouse	Ghost of Keeper Joshua Card
Fort Constitution	Ghost of children obscure photos taken in the fort

Rhode Island

Southeast Light, Block Island	Ghost of "Mad Maggie"

Ghost Ships Seen at	**Ghost Ship's Name**
Harpswell, Maine	Dash – The "Ship of Death"
New Haven, Connecticut	"Great Shippe" in the Sky
Salem, Massachusetts	"Noah's Dove"
Block Island, Rhode Island	"Palatine" a/k/a The Princess Augusta

Haunted Ships and Forts

USS Constitution	Most Haunted Ship in the World
Fort Strong	The Woman in Red
Fort Warren	The Lady in Black
Fort Independence	Walled up Christmas Day duelist
Fort Knox	Ghost of Custer's Ordnance Sergeant
Fort William Henry	Haunted by the ghost of an Indian Chief
Fort Wetherill	Ghost of a Demon Dog
Fort Adams	Tunnels of Terror
USS Salem	Stored 400+ corpses in its freezer
Col Jonathan Buck Statue	Cursed founder speaks from his coffin - "Close the lid son"

Other Books by Ted Burbank

The Golden Age of Piracy on Cape Cod and in New England

Cape Cod Shipwrecks - *"Graveyard of the Atlantic"*

Pirates and Treasure on Cape Cod

Shipwrecks, Pirates and Treasure in Maine

A Homeowner's Complete Guide to Energy Independence

The "Islands" of Ocean Bluff and Brant Rock

365 Ways to Unplug Your Kids or *How to have fun without TV or Computers*

A Guide to Plymouth's Famous Burial Hill

Any of these books can be ordered from Salty Pilgrim Press by going to www.SaltyPilgrim.com

Need an entertaining and interesting speaker?

Ted is available to provide your club or organization a presentation based upon any of the subjects covered by his books or to participant in your Pirate Festival or Fair.
Call: 508.794.1200 to schedule

Ted Burbank

Considering Selling or Buying a Business?

Go to www.BuySellBiz.com for some of the valuable information and tips Ted gained through participating in the purchase and sale of more than 2,000 private businesses

Made in the USA
Charleston, SC
06 August 2015